Copyright © 2023 by Will

All rights reserved. No p.
retrieval system, or transmitted in any form or by any means, electronic, mechanical, photocopying, recording, or otherwise, without the prior written permission of the publisher.

This book is a work of fiction. Names, characters, businesses, organizations, places, events, and incidents either are the product of the author's imagination or are used fictitiously. Any resemblance to actual persons, living or dead, events, or locales is entirely coincidental.

ISBN:9798375052786
First edition, 2023

Disclaimer: The information contained in this book is for general information purposes only. The information is provided by the author and while we endeavor to keep the information up to date and correct, we make no representations or warranties of any kind, express or implied, about the completeness, accuracy, reliability, suitability or availability with respect to the book or the information, products, services, or related graphics contained in the book for any purpose. Any reliance you place on such information is therefore strictly at your own risk.

Unlock your Power

Stress, stress, stress. It seems like it's all we ever hear about these days. And let's be real, it's not exactly a walk in the park. We're all familiar with the feeling of being overwhelmed, anxious, or even depressed when facing stress. It's like a never-ending cycle of worry and chaos. But don't worry, you're not alone. We've all been there.

I remember when I first started feeling the effects of stress on my daily life. I was constantly tired, had trouble sleeping and even gained weight. I couldn't focus, my productivity was down and I felt irritable all the time. I knew I had to do something about it, but where to start? That's when I decided to start experimenting with different techniques to manage stress, and let me tell you, it's been a game-changer.

In this book, I want to share with you all the techniques and methods that have helped me to take control of my thoughts and emotions, and improve my overall well-being. From mindfulness and meditation to exercise and nature, you will discover a variety of methods that you can use to manage stress in your own life. And the best part? They're all based on techniques that I've personally tried and found to be effective. So, whether you're a busy working professional, a stay-at-home parent, or a student, this book has something for everyone.

Managing stress and staying focused is important for so many reasons, and let me tell you, it's not just about being able to handle a busy schedule. Stress can have a negative impact on our physical, mental and emotional well-being. It can lead to chronic health issues such as heart disease and high blood pressure, as well as mental health conditions like anxiety and depression. It can also affect our relationships, productivity and overall quality of life.

But it's not always easy to stay focused and manage stress. It's like trying to catch a wild horse, it's hard and sometimes it feels impossible. But with the right tools and techniques, we can learn how to tame the wild horse and take control of our stress and focus.

Imagine being able to fall asleep at night without worrying about everything on your to-do list. Imagine being able to handle a difficult situation without your heart racing. Imagine being able to focus on the task at hand and getting things done efficiently. It's like a dream come true, right?

And let's not forget the added bonus of being able to enjoy the little things in life. Imagine being able to enjoy a cup of coffee without feeling jittery. Imagine being able to enjoy a good book without feeling guilty for not doing something else. Imagine being able to enjoy a good belly laugh without feeling guilty about it. It's like the cherry on top of a sundae.

In this book, I'll share with you my personal experiences and the techniques that have helped me to manage stress and improve focus in my daily life. It's not just about surviving, it's about thriving. So, let's take control of our stress and start living our best lives.

Mindfulness

Welcome to the world of mindfulness! Are you ready to give your brain a spa day? Mindfulness is the practice of paying attention to your thoughts, feelings, and bodily sensations without judgment. It's like a secret weapon for stress management. It's like a ninja technique for your brain.

Now, I know what you're thinking, "But wait, I'm already paying attention to my thoughts and feelings, that's why I'm stressed in the first place!" And you're right, but mindfulness is different. It's not about getting rid of your thoughts or feelings, it's about observing them without judgment. It's like being a scientist observing an experiment, you're not trying to change the outcome, you're just observing it.

Let me give you an example. Have you ever been in a situation where you're so caught up in your thoughts and emotions that you can't focus on what's happening in the present moment? Like when you're in a meeting and your mind is wandering to that thing you need to do later, or when you're on a date and you're thinking about your ex. Mindfulness can help you to snap out of that and bring your attention back to the present moment. It's like hitting the reset button on your brain.

But it's not just about being present in the moment, mindfulness has been shown to have a positive impact on physical and mental health. It can help to reduce stress, anxiety, and depression, improve overall well-being, and even help with chronic pain. It's like hitting the jackpot for your brain and body.

In this chapter, we'll explore the practice of mindfulness in more detail and discover how you can use it to manage stress in your daily life. We'll talk about different mindfulness techniques and provide practical tips and examples for incorporating them into your daily routine. So, let's get started on giving your brain that spa day it deserves!

Mindfulness is a powerful tool for managing stress and improving overall well-being. It's the practice of paying attention to your thoughts, feelings, and bodily sensations without judgment. It's about being present in the moment, rather than getting lost in worries about the past or future. It's like a spa day for your brain, a mental massage if you will.

But how exactly does it work? Well, let's dive into the science behind mindfulness. Mindfulness has been shown to activate certain areas of the brain, such as the prefrontal cortex, which is responsible for regulating emotions and attention. It also decreases activity in the amygdala, which is responsible for the stress response. In other words, mindfulness helps to turn down the volume on our stress response and improves our ability to focus and regulate our emotions. It's like having a personal DJ for your brain, controlling the playlist of your thoughts.

But enough about the science, let's talk about how mindfulness can be applied in our daily lives. One of the most popular mindfulness techniques is meditation. Meditation is like a mental workout; it helps to train your brain to focus and become more aware of your thoughts and emotions. It's like hitting the gym for your brain, making it stronger and more resilient.

Another mindfulness technique is mindful breathing. It's a simple yet powerful technique that can be done anywhere, anytime. It's like a mental pause button, it helps to calm the mind and reduce stress. It's like a mental chill pill for your brain.

Mindful walking is another technique that can be used to practice mindfulness in daily life. It's like taking a mental vacation while walking. It helps to reduce stress and improve focus. It's like a mental vacation for your brain, a mini-getaway from the daily stressors of life.

1. Breathe consciously

When you're standing in line at the grocery store, waiting what feels like an eternity to check out, it's easy to let your mind wander and start stressing about all the things on your to-do list. But what if I told you that there's a way to make that wait feel a little less... well, stressful? Enter mindful breathing.

Now, I know what you're thinking. "But I've been breathing my entire life, what's the big deal?" Well, my friend, it's all about the way you breathe. Mindful breathing is all about being present in the moment and paying attention to the sensation of your breath. It's like giving your mind a little break from all the chaos and noise of daily life.

So next time you're stuck in line at the grocery store, take a deep breath in through your nose and out through your mouth. Pay attention to the way the air feels as it enters and exits your body. And if you really want to take it to the next level, try counting to four as you inhale and counting to four as you exhale. This will help slow down your breath and bring a sense of calm to your mind and body.

Now, I know this might sound a little "woo-woo" to some of you, but trust me, it works. You might even find yourself looking forward to waiting in line at the grocery store just so you can practice your mindful breathing. Plus, think about it this way: if you can find a sense of peace and calm while waiting in line at the grocery store, imagine what you can do when you're facing bigger stressors in your life. So go ahead, give it a try. Your mind (and your grocery list) will thank you.

2. Nature: enjoy the wonders of wildlife

When it comes to reducing daily stress, one of the best things you can do is take a mindful walk-in nature. Not only does being in nature have a calming effect on the mind and body, but by focusing on the sights, sounds, and smells of your surroundings, you can really immerse yourself in the present moment and let go of any stress or worries you may be carrying with you.

One of the great things about a mindful walk-in nature is that it can be done anywhere. Whether you live in a bustling city or a quiet rural area, there's bound to be a park or nature reserve nearby that you can explore. So, lace up your hiking boots, grab your water bottle, and hit the trails.

As you walk, take in the sights around you. Notice the different shades of green on the leaves of the trees, the way the sunlight filters through the branches, and the way the birds flit from tree to tree. Listen to the sound of the wind rustling through the leaves, the sound of a nearby stream, and the distant calls of animals. And smell the fresh, clean air, the damp earth, and the scent of nearby flowers or plants.

You'll find that as you focus on these things, your mind will naturally start to relax and let go of any stress or worries you may be carrying. And as you continue to walk, you'll start to feel more and more at peace.

Of course, a mindful walk-in nature isn't just about reducing stress, it's also a great way to get some exercise and fresh air, which can have a positive impact on your overall health and well-being. So, grab your backpack and hit the trails for a nature-filled stress-busting walk today!

3. Savour every bite

Eating mindfully may seem like a small change, but it can have a big impact on reducing stress. Imagine sitting down to a delicious meal, but instead of mindlessly shoveling food into your mouth while scrolling through your phone, you take the time to really savor each bite. Pay attention to the flavors and textures of your food, and enjoy the experience of eating.

It may sound simple, but this small shift in focus can help to alleviate stress by bringing you into the present moment and allowing you to fully enjoy your food. Plus, when you're more mindful about what you're eating, you may find yourself making healthier choices and even losing weight!

We all know that the best part of mindful eating is getting to indulge in that extra piece of cake or second helping of mashed potatoes without feeling guilty about it. So go ahead and treat yourself, just make sure to savor every bite and enjoy the moment!

Also, you can use this technique when you eat at work and take a break, it will help you to avoid stress and enjoy your meal more.

Mindful eating is a great way to reduce stress and enjoy your food more. Next time you sit down to a meal, put away your phone, pay attention to your food, and savor each bite. Your taste buds (and your stress levels) will thank you.

4. Use a guided meditation app during your morning commute

When it comes to reducing daily stress, one of the simplest and most effective ways is to use a guided meditation app during your morning commute on public transportation. Whether you're taking the bus or the train, the morning commute can be a hectic and stressful time. With so many people crowded together in a confined space, it's easy to get caught up in the hustle and bustle and start feeling anxious and stressed. But by using a guided meditation app, you can turn your morning commute into a peaceful and stress-free experience.

Imagine closing your eyes, putting on your headphones, and being guided through a relaxing meditation as you make your way to work or school. You'll be able to focus on your breath, let go of racing thoughts, and tune out the noise and distractions around you. By the time you arrive at your destination, you'll feel calm, centered, and ready to take on the day. And the best part is, you can do this all without ever leaving your seat!

But it's not just the morning commute where you can use this technique, you can use it whenever you're stuck in a crowded place or in a stressful situation. The next time you're at the doctor's office, or a long line at the store, or even stuck in traffic, take a deep breath and use a guided meditation app to help you stay calm and focused.

You can even try to make it a game, try to see how long you can stay focus and how deep you can go in the meditation, and reward yourself when you achieve a good score. It will also help you to improve your ability to focus and to be more mindful in your daily life.

So next time you're feeling stressed and frazzled during your morning commute, don't let it get the best of you. Instead, use a guided meditation app to take control of your stress and start your day off on the right foot. Trust me, you'll be glad you did.

5. Practice attentive listening during meetings at work

When it comes to work, it can be easy to get caught up in your own thoughts and worries. Meetings can turn into a mental battlefield, with everyone fighting for their own agenda and ideas. But what if there was a way to clear your mind and focus on the present moment during these meetings? Enter mindful listening.

By actively listening to others and being present in the moment, you can reduce the amount of stress and mental clutter that comes with meetings. Instead of worrying about what you're going to say next or how you're going to push your own agenda, you can focus on what others are saying and truly hear their ideas.

But how do you practice mindful listening? It's simple, but not always easy. Start by setting an intention before the meeting to be present and listen actively. Then, when the meeting starts, focus on the speaker's words and body language. Try to eliminate distractions, such as your phone or other electronic devices, and avoid interrupting or planning your response while the other person is speaking.

By practicing mindful listening, you'll be able to reduce stress and be more productive during meetings. It's a win-win situation. And who knows, you might even learn something new or come up with a creative solution that you never would have thought of otherwise. So next time you're sitting in a meeting, take a deep breath and give mindful listening a try. Your mind (and colleagues) will thank you.

6. Yoga

When it comes to managing stress, yoga is like a superhero in disguise. It's a gentle and effective way to improve focus and reduce stress before bedtime. The combination of physical movement and mindfulness can be a powerful stress-buster.

Think about it, you're contorting your body into different shapes, all while focusing on your breath and being present in the moment. It's like giving your mind and body a full-body massage, leaving you feeling relaxed and rejuvenated.

Plus, yoga is a great way to unwind before bedtime. It helps to quiet the mind and release any tension in the body, making it easier to fall asleep. And who doesn't love a good night's sleep?

But don't just take my word for it, give it a try yourself. Whether it's a quick 10-minute flow or a longer class, make yoga a part of your bedtime routine. Who knows, you may even find yourself sleeping like a baby.

And let's not forget about the added bonus, you'll also improve your flexibility, balance and strength. So, it's like killing two birds with one stone. It's the ultimate win-win situation. So, roll out your mat, put on some comfortable clothes, and let the stress melt away. Namaste!

7. Practice mindfulness during your daily shower

When you're in the shower, it's easy to zone out and let your mind wander to all the things you need to do, or the stress you're feeling. But what if I told you that your daily shower could be a tool for reducing stress instead? All you have to do is practice mindfulness during your shower.

Instead of letting your mind wander, bring your attention to the sensation of the water on your skin. Feel the warmth as it runs down your body, and pay attention to the sensation of the water as it hits different parts of your skin. Notice the way the water feels on your scalp, and the way it drips down your face. If you're using soap or shampoo, pay attention to the way the lather feels on your skin and the scent of the product.

This simple act of mindfulness can help you to focus on the present moment and let go of the stress and worries of the day. It's like hitting the reset button for your mind and body. And who doesn't love a good shower? So the next time you're in the shower, try to bring your focus to the sensation of the water on your skin, and see if it helps to reduce your stress levels. Who knows, it might even become your favorite part of your daily routine.

8. Write a diary

Incorporating mindful journaling into your daily routine is a great way to reduce daily stress. It's like having a personal therapist that you can access anytime and anywhere. By reflecting on your thoughts and emotions before bed, you're able to process any lingering stress from the day and release it before falling asleep. Plus, it's a great opportunity to give yourself some self-care and gratitude.

Just imagine, at the end of a long day, you get to sit down with a cup of tea (or a glass of wine, we don't judge!) and write about all the things you're grateful for. It's like hitting the mental reset button before bed. Not only will you fall asleep feeling more relaxed and at peace, but you'll also wake up with a fresh perspective and a clearer mind.

So go ahead, grab a journal and start jotting down those thoughts and emotions. You'll be amazed at how much better you'll feel after just a few nights of mindful journaling.

9. Use mindfulness to improve your sleep

Going to bed with a racing mind can be one of the most frustrating things in the world. It's like trying to fall asleep with a never-ending to-do list running through your head. But what if I told you that there's a simple solution to this problem? Mindfulness can help you fall asleep faster and sleep better.

One of the simplest ways to practice mindfulness before bed is by focusing on your breath. As you lay in bed, try to pay attention to the sensation of the air moving in and out of your body. This can help to calm your mind and let go of any racing thoughts.

You can also try to focus on any bodily sensations you may be feeling, such as the feeling of your sheets against your skin or the sound of your breath. This can help to bring your attention to the present moment and away from the stress of the day.

Another way to practice mindfulness before bed is by doing a "brain dump" journaling session. Before you go to bed, take a few minutes to write down any thoughts or worries that may be keeping you up at night. This can help to get them out of your head and onto the page, allowing you to let go of them and fall asleep more easily.

But the best part about incorporating mindfulness into your bedtime routine is the improvement in sleep quality. By focusing on the present moment and letting go of racing thoughts, you'll be able to fall asleep faster and stay asleep longer. So next time you're lying in bed with a racing mind, try out some mindfulness techniques and see how it can help you drift off into dreamland.

10. Practice multitasking

When it comes to managing stress, multitasking can often feel like a double-edged sword. On one hand, it can feel productive to juggle multiple tasks at once. But on the other hand, it can be easy to get lost in the whirlwind of switching back and forth between tasks, leaving you feeling frazzled and stressed out. But fear not, my friend! Mindful multitasking is here to save the day.

First things first, let's redefine multitasking. Instead of trying to do a million things at once, mindful multitasking is all about focusing on one task at a time. By giving each task your undivided attention, you'll be able to complete it more efficiently and with less stress.

Now, I know what you're thinking. "But wait, isn't multitasking supposed to be efficient? Won't this take longer?" And to that, I say, not necessarily! Sure, it may take a bit of practice to get used to this new way of working, but once you get the hang of it, you'll find that you're able to complete tasks more quickly and with less stress.

But how exactly do you practice mindful multitasking? One way is to use the Pomodoro Technique. This technique involves breaking your tasks into 25-minute intervals with short breaks in between. During each interval, focus solely on one task. By giving your full attention to one task at a time, you'll be able to complete it more efficiently and with less stress.

Another way to practice mindful multitasking is to set boundaries for yourself. For example, if you're working on a task, turn off your phone or put it in another room. This will help you to stay focused on the task at hand and avoid getting lost in distractions.

Incorporating mindful multitasking into your daily routine can be a game-changer when it comes to managing stress. So next time you're feeling overwhelmed by all the tasks on your plate, remember to take a step back, focus on one task at a time and practice mindful multitasking.

11. Stay present and focused during your sports training

Looking to reduce daily stress while also improving your performance in sports or physical activities? Look no further than mindfulness! By staying present and focused during training, you can not only improve your performance but also leave your stress behind.

Think about it, when you're in the zone during a workout, you're not thinking about that deadline at work or the fight you had with your significant other. You're focused on the task at hand, and that's where mindfulness comes in. It's all about being present in the moment, and what better way to do that than through physical activity?

But don't just take my word for it, try it out for yourself. Next time you're at the gym or on the field, take a deep breath and focus on your body, your movements, and how it feels to push yourself to the limit. Pay attention to the sensation of your muscles working and the sound of your breath. Trust me, it's a game-changer.

And the best part? You'll not only feel less stressed but you'll also see improvements in your physical performance. It's a win-win situation. So, next time you're working out, ditch the distractions and focus on the present moment. Your stress and your performance will thank you.

12. Improve your concentration during your revisions

Are you tired of feeling like your mind is scattered and unfocused while studying? Well, let me introduce you to the power of mindfulness. By breaking down your study sessions into shorter periods and incorporating mindful breaks, you'll be able to focus better and retain more information. Imagine being able to ace that exam without pulling an all-nighter!

But how does mindfulness improve concentration, you may ask? It's simple. Mindfulness is all about being present in the moment and focusing on one task at a time. So, instead of trying to juggle multiple tasks at once, you'll be able to give your full attention to the task at hand. We all know how easy it is to get lost in distractions like social media or Netflix. But with mindfulness, you'll be able to stay on track and get more done in less time.

But don't just take my word for it, give it a try yourself. Next time you sit down to study, set a timer for 25 minutes and focus solely on the task at hand. When the timer goes off, take a 5-minute mindful break to clear your mind and refocus. Repeat this cycle and watch as your concentration and productivity soar.

So, don't let stress and distractions get in the way of your studies. Incorporate mindfulness and watch as you become the master of focus and concentration.

13. Pay attention to your surroundings when walking to work or school

Are you familiar with the concept of "mindful walking"? It's a simple, yet powerful technique for reducing stress and increasing mindfulness. The idea is to take a walk outside, and instead of allowing your mind to wander or be preoccupied with your thoughts, you focus on the present moment and all the sights, sounds, and sensations around you.

When it comes to incorporating mindfulness into your daily routine, taking a mindful walk on your way to work or school is a great place to start. Instead of rushing to your destination, try to focus on the sensation of your feet hitting the pavement, the sound of birds chirping, or the smell of freshly cut grass.

By paying attention to your surroundings, you'll find that you're more present and less stressed. Not only that, but you'll also start to appreciate the small things in life that often go unnoticed. It's like turning off the noise of the world and tuning into a different frequency.

So, next time you're walking to work or school, don't just rush to your destination. Take a mindful walk, and see how much better you feel. And if anyone gives you strange looks, just tell them you're doing a stress reduction technique. They'll probably think you're some kind of Zen master.

14. Manage your chronic pain

One of the most effective ways to manage chronic pain is by incorporating mindfulness into your daily routine. Instead of simply trying to ignore or push through the pain, mindfulness allows you to pay attention to the sensations in your body and to learn how to work with them in a more effective way.

Practicing mindfulness as a tool for managing chronic pain is like taking a step back and really observing the pain, without judging it or trying to change it. It's like being a scientist studying a specimen in a lab, you're simply observing without trying to manipulate it. By paying attention to the sensations in your body, you start to understand the patterns and triggers that cause your pain.

One of the best things about using mindfulness as a tool for managing chronic pain is that it can help to reduce pain and improve quality of life without the need for medication. So, next time you feel a twinge of pain, instead of reaching for the ibuprofen, try taking a mindful approach and see if it makes a difference.

And who doesn't love a good science lab analogy? So, put on your lab coat, grab your microscope and start observing the pain, you might be surprised by what you find.

15. Practice mindful parenting by being present and attentive with your children

Parenting can be stressful, there's no denying that. But what if I told you that you could turn that stress into a positive experience? By incorporating mindfulness into your parenting, you can not only improve your relationship with your children, but also reduce your daily stress.

Imagine playing a game with your child, but instead of being preoccupied with your to-do list or worrying about the future, you're fully present in the moment. You're fully engaged with your child, savoring every laugh and smile. That's the power of mindful parenting.

But it's not just about playing games, mindfulness can be incorporated into every aspect of parenting. From bath time to bedtime, you can focus on the present moment and truly enjoy the time with your child.

And the best part? Not only will you feel less stressed, but your child will also benefit from your presence and attention. It's a win-win situation.

So, next time your child wants to play a game, put down your phone, take a deep breath and let the stress go. It's time to enjoy the little things in life, and what better way to do that than with your little ones

16. Manage your stress during pregnancy

Let's face it, pregnancy can be a rollercoaster of emotions and stress. From the constant worry about the health of your baby to the physical changes happening in your body, it can be a lot to handle. But don't fret, there's a simple and effective solution to help manage it all - mindfulness.

By incorporating mindfulness practices into your daily routine, you can help reduce stress and anxiety during pregnancy. One way to do this is by focusing on your breath and bodily sensations. The next time you feel a wave of stress coming on, take a deep breath in and out, and pay attention to the sensation of the air entering and leaving your body. This simple practice can help calm your mind and reduce stress.

Another way to use mindfulness during pregnancy is by paying attention to your surroundings. Take a mindful walk in nature and focus on the sights, sounds, and smells of your surroundings. As you walk, pay attention to the sensation of your feet hitting the ground, the sound of birds chirping, and the smell of fresh grass. This can help to ground you in the present moment and reduce stress.

But it's not just about the physical practices, mindfulness can also help improve the overall well-being of both mother and baby. By focusing on the present moment and letting go of worries about the future or regrets about the past, you can create a more peaceful and positive environment for both you and your little one.

So, don't let stress take over during your pregnancy. Incorporate mindfulness practices into your daily routine and watch as it helps to reduce stress and improve overall well-being for both you and your baby. And remember, it's not about being a perfect parent, it's about being a mindful one.

17. Take care of your skin

Are you feeling stressed out and looking for a new way to relax and unwind? Look no further than incorporating mindfulness into your daily skincare routine! No, I'm not talking about applying face masks and cucumbers to your eyes (although that does sound pretty relaxing), I'm talking about paying attention to the sensation of the products on your skin.

Next time you're applying your moisturizer or face wash, take a moment to really focus on the feeling of the product on your skin. Notice the coolness of the cream as it glides on, or the gentle tingling sensation of a face scrub. By paying attention to these small details, you're able to fully immerse yourself in the present moment and let go of any racing thoughts or stress.

Plus, by being more mindful during your skincare routine, you'll be able to better understand your skin's needs and find the right products for you. Who knew that a simple act of washing your face could have such a big impact on your overall well-being? So go ahead, give it a try and watch as your stress levels (and your skin!) start to improve. And if all else fails, you can always fall back on the cucumber-on-eyes technique, I won't judge.

18. Practice gardening

Are you ready to get your green thumb on and leave stress behind? Incorporating mindfulness into your daily gardening routine can be a game-changer. Imagine yourself in your backyard or on your balcony, surrounded by lush greenery and the sweet scent of blooming flowers. As you tend to your plants, take a moment to focus on the sensation of the soil between your fingers, the smell of the plants, and the sound of the birds chirping in the background.

Gardening is like a form of therapy, a way to connect with nature and clear your mind. By paying attention to the small details and the present moment, you'll find yourself feeling more relaxed and at peace. So go ahead, plant some seeds, and watch them grow, and as they grow, your stress will shrink.

Also, don't forget to take a moment to appreciate the beauty of your garden and give yourself a pat on the back for creating something beautiful and living, also it's a great way to make sure you are getting your daily dose of Vitamin D and fresh air.

So, the next time you feel stressed, head outside and get your hands dirty. Happy gardening!

19. Set limits with technology

Are you tired of feeling chained to your phone, constantly checking notifications and scrolling through social media? Fear not, my friend, for mindfulness is here to help you break free from the shackles of technology and improve your relationship with it.

By incorporating mindfulness into your daily routine, you can set boundaries and truly be present in the moment without distractions. Instead of mindlessly scrolling through Instagram during your lunch break, take a mindful walk outside and pay attention to your surroundings. Instead of answering emails late at night, set a designated time for checking and responding to them and use the rest of the evening to unwind and relax.

Not only will this improve your relationship with technology, but it will also reduce your daily stress levels. So, put down the phone, step away from the computer, and give mindfulness a try.

20. Pet your furry friends

If you're looking for a way to reduce daily stress, consider incorporating the practice of mindful petting into your routine. This can be done by simply taking a few minutes each day to focus on the sensation of your furry friend's fur and breath as you pet them.

Think about it, have you ever been petting your cat or dog and not even noticed that you've been doing it for 20 minutes? It's easy to get lost in the soothing sensation of their soft fur, the sound of their purring or the rhythm of their breathing. This is the perfect opportunity to practice mindfulness, by being present in the moment and focusing solely on the sensation of petting your furry friend.

And who doesn't love a good petting session with their furry buddy? It's a win-win situation for both you and your pet. You get to reduce stress and they get to be loved and feel close to you. Plus, it's a great opportunity to bond with your pet and strengthen your relationship with them.

And if you don't have a pet, you can always visit a friend's, volunteer at a pet shelter or even just watch some cat videos on youtube. The point is, taking a moment to focus on the present and the sensation of petting, can be incredibly beneficial for reducing stress and improving overall well-being. So go ahead, give your furry friend some love and let them help you reduce stress in your life.

Exercise

Regular physical activity is like a superhero for your stress levels. It's like having your own personal stress-fighting team, and let me tell you, they're pretty darn good at their job. But how exactly does it work?

First off, let's talk about the science behind it. When you engage in physical activity, your body releases endorphins, also known as "feel-good" hormones. These endorphins can help to improve mood and reduce feelings of stress and anxiety. It's like having your own personal happiness squad, cheering you on every step of the way.

Physical activity can also help to reduce the physical symptoms of stress, such as tension headaches and muscle aches. It's like having your own personal massage therapist, working out the kinks and knots in your body.

But it's not just about the short-term benefits. Regular physical activity can also have long-term benefits for stress management. It can help to improve sleep quality, boost self-esteem, and increase feelings of overall well-being. It's like having your own personal personal trainer, helping you to become the best version of yourself.

Sometimes the thought of hitting the gym or going for a run can feel like the last thing you want to do when you're feeling stressed. That's why it's important to find an activity that you enjoy, whether it's dancing, swimming, or even just going for a walk. It's like having your own personal party planner, making sure you're having fun while you're working out.

And the best part is, you don't have to be a marathon runner or fitness guru to experience the benefits of regular physical activity. Even just a small amount of exercise can make a big difference. It's like having your own personal cheer squad, cheering you on no matter how small the victory.

So, if you're feeling stressed, don't hesitate to lace up those shoes and hit the pavement. Or the dance floor. Or the pool. Whatever activity you choose, know that you're doing something great for your body and mind. It's like having your own personal stress-fighting team, and they're always ready to help you out.

21. Running

Running is one of the most effective ways to reduce stress and improve your overall well-being. Not only does it provide a physical outlet for pent-up energy, but it also releases endorphins, known as the "feel-good" hormones, that can help boost your mood and reduce feelings of stress.

When you're feeling overwhelmed and stressed, going for a run can be like putting your brain in the washing machine. All of the dirt and grime of stress is washed away as you pound the pavement, leaving you feeling refreshed and rejuvenated. The repetitive motion of running can also be meditative, allowing you to focus on your breath and let go of racing thoughts.

One of the best things about running is that it's a low-cost and accessible form of exercise. All you need is a good pair of shoes and some comfortable clothes. You can run outside and take in the sights and sounds of nature, or hit the treadmill at your local gym.

But running isn't just about the physical benefits, it's also a great way to clear your mind and improve your mental well-being. So, next time you're feeling stressed, lace up your running shoes and hit the pavement. You'll be surprised at how much better you'll feel after a good run.

22. Yoga

When it comes to reducing daily stress, yoga is a fantastic option to consider. Not only does it focus on physical movement and flexibility, but it also incorporates mindfulness and breath work to help calm the mind and release tension in the body.

Think of yoga as a full-body massage for your mind and body. You'll twist, bend and stretch your way to a more relaxed and rejuvenated state. Imagine all the stress and tension in your body being kneaded out like dough, leaving you feeling like a brand new person.

But yoga isn't just about the physical aspect, it's also about connecting with your breath and finding inner peace. By focusing on your breath and movements, you'll be able to let go of racing thoughts and distractions, allowing you to fully immerse yourself in the present moment.

So, if you're looking to reduce daily stress, roll out your yoga mat and get ready to bend over backwards to leave stress behind.

23. Swimming

Imagine diving into the pool and feeling the cool water envelop you. As you start to swim, you feel your muscles begin to relax, and your mind starts to clear. The sensation of weightlessness that comes with swimming is like taking a mental vacation. You're free from the weight of your stress, and you're able to focus solely on the sensation of the water on your skin and the rhythm of your breath.

Swimming is not only a great physical workout, but it's also a great way to reduce stress and improve your mental well-being. It's like hitting the reset button on your mind and body, leaving you feeling refreshed and rejuvenated. So, next time you're feeling overwhelmed by stress, take a dip in the pool and let the water wash away all your worries. Who knows, you might even come out feeling like a mermaid or merman, ready to take on the world with a clear and calm mind.

24. Dancing

Are you looking for a fun and effective way to reduce stress and improve your overall well-being? Look no further than dancing!

Dancing is a great way to let loose and forget about your worries for a little while. It's like a party for your body and mind, and stress isn't invited. Whether you're a professional dancer or have two left feet, dancing is an accessible and enjoyable way to improve your physical and mental health.

When you dance, you're not just moving your body, you're also releasing endorphins, which are the "feel-good" chemicals in your brain. These endorphins can help to reduce stress and improve your mood. Dancing also improves your cardiovascular health, increases flexibility and balance, and can even boost your confidence.

You don't need any special equipment or a gym membership to start dancing. You can dance in the comfort of your own home, put on some music and let the beat guide you. You can also join a dance class or club to learn different styles and meet new people.

So, next time you're feeling stressed, put on your favorite song and let your body move to the beat. Dancing is the perfect way to leave your stress behind and have fun at the same time. So, put on your dancing shoes and get ready to shake, shimmy, and sweat away your stress!

25. Weightlifting

Weightlifting is a great way to reduce stress and improve overall well-being. The physical act of lifting weights can be therapeutic, allowing you to focus on the task at hand and forget about the stressors in your life. Plus, the endorphins released during a workout can give you a boost of energy and leave you feeling euphoric.

Think of weightlifting as a form of stress management. It's like squeezing a stress ball, except it's your muscles that are getting a workout, and your stress level drops. Imagine all your worries and troubles being lifted away with each rep. By the end of your workout, you'll not only have a stronger body but also a clearer mind.

But weightlifting isn't just about looking good, it's about feeling good too. It's a form of self-care that can help you manage your stress levels, improve your mood and boost your self-confidence.

So why not give it a try? You don't need to be a bodybuilder to benefit from weightlifting. Whether you're a beginner or a pro, there's always a weightlifting routine that's right for you. And the best part? You don't need to lift heavy weights to see the benefits. Even a light workout can help reduce stress and improve your overall well-being. So grab a pair of dumbbells, pump some iron and pump out that stress!

26. Cycling

Cycling is a great way to reduce daily stress and improve your overall well-being. It's like a mini-vacation for your mind and body, allowing you to escape the daily grind and clear your head. Imagine pedaling away from all your worries, taking in the sights, and feeling the wind in your hair. It's like a mental detox, leaving you feeling refreshed and rejuvenated.

One of the best things about cycling is that it can be done anywhere. Whether you're in the city or out in the countryside, there's always a new route to explore. You can cycle to work, to the store, or just for fun. It's a low-impact form of exercise that's easy on the joints and perfect for people of all ages and fitness levels.

Cycling is also a great way to meet new people and make friends. Joining a cycling group or club can be a great way to socialize and connect with like-minded people. It's also a great way to explore new places and discover hidden gems in your area.

But perhaps the best thing about cycling is how it makes you feel. It's a natural mood booster that can help to reduce stress, anxiety and depression. It's like hitting the reset button on your brain and leaving all your worries behind.

So, why not give it a try? Get yourself a bike and hit the road. You'll be amazed at how much better you feel after a good ride. Just remember to wear a helmet, and don't forget to stop and take in the sights along the way. After all, that's half the fun!

27. Hiking

Are you feeling overwhelmed with stress and in need of a mental and physical cleanse? Well, let me tell you, my friend, hiking is the answer to all your problems. Forget about expensive spa days or fancy yoga classes, all you need is a pair of comfortable shoes and a scenic trail.

Hiking is like hitting the reset button on your mind and body. As soon as you step onto the trail, you leave all your stress and worries behind. The fresh air, beautiful scenery, and the sound of nature all work together to create a serene and peaceful environment. It's like a giant stress vacuum, sucking up all the toxins of daily life and leaving you feeling refreshed and rejuvenated.

But hiking isn't just good for your mental health, it's also great for your physical well-being. It's a full-body workout that gets your blood pumping and your muscles working. Plus, it's a great way to get some much-needed Vitamin D from the sun. Who knew that reducing stress could be so easy and enjoyable?

And let's not forget about the added bonus of getting a killer Instagram picture at the top of the trail. Who wouldn't want to show off their hard work and stunning views to all their friends and followers?

28. Pilates

Are you tired of feeling stressed and overwhelmed? Do you long for a way to reset both your mind and body? Look no further, my friend, because Pilates is the answer to all your problems. Forget about expensive spa days or complicated yoga routines, all you need is a mat and a positive attitude.

Pilates is like hitting the refresh button on your mind and body. As soon as you start your routine, you leave all your stress and worries behind. The controlled movements and deep breathing work together to create a serene and peaceful environment, allowing you to focus on the present moment and let go of any negative thoughts. It's like a mental and physical cleanse, getting rid of all the toxins of stress.

But Pilates isn't just good for your mental health, it's also great for your physical well-being. It's a full-body workout that targets your core, improves your flexibility, and increases your overall strength. Plus, it's a low-impact workout that is suitable for people of all ages and fitness levels. Who knew that reducing stress could be so easy and enjoyable?

And let's not forget about the added bonus of having a strong core and a toned body. Who wouldn't want to look and feel their best while reducing their stress levels?

29. Rock Climbing

Well, let me tell you, rock climbing is the perfect way to scale new heights and leave stress behind.

For me, rock climbing is not just a physical activity, but a mental escape. As soon as I step into the climbing gym, all my worries and stress disappear, replaced by the focus and determination required to conquer each climb.

It's a full-body workout that challenges me physically, but it's also a mental workout as I have to strategize and problem solve my way up the wall. Plus, reaching the top and looking down from the summit is an indescribable feeling of accomplishment and it makes all the hard work worth it.

But it's not just about the physical and mental benefits, rock climbing also has a social aspect. It's a great way to bond with friends and make new ones, as you all work together to conquer the wall. And let's not forget the sense of community and belonging that comes with being part of the climbing scene.

30. Zumba

This high-energy dance workout is like a stress-busting party where your worries can't keep up with the beat.

As soon as you start shaking, shimmying, and sweating to the lively Latin-inspired music, you'll forget all about your daily stresses. The combination of upbeat music, energizing moves, and the endorphins released during exercise, make for an unbeatable stress-relieving combination. It's like a mental and physical reset, leaving you feeling refreshed and rejuvenated.

But Zumba isn't just good for your mental health, it's also great for your physical well-being. It's a full-body workout that will get your heart pumping and your muscles working. Plus, it's a fun and enjoyable way to stay active and burn calories. Who knew that reducing stress could be so much fun?

Dancing with a group of like-minded individuals is a great way to bond and make new friends.

The energy and enthusiasm of the instructor and class will leave you feeling uplifted and inspired.

31. Tai Chi

Are you looking for a way to reduce stress and find inner peace? Look no further than Tai Chi. This ancient Chinese martial art is like a moving meditation, where you focus on your breath and your movements, leaving stress behind.

As soon as you start practicing Tai Chi, you'll find yourself in a state of relaxation and tranquility. The slow, fluid movements and deep breathing techniques help to calm the mind and release tension in the body. It's like a mental and physical reset, leaving you feeling refreshed and rejuvenated, a peaceful journey for your mind and body.

But Tai Chi isn't just good for your mental health, it's also great for your physical well-being. The gentle and low-impact movements help to improve balance, flexibility, and coordination.

It's a great way to improve your overall fitness, without putting too much stress on your body.

32. CrossFit

Well, let me tell you, CrossFit is the ultimate stress-busting workout. It's like hitting the reset button on your stress levels, leaving you feeling strong and energized.

As soon as you step into the box and start lifting weights, doing cardio, and sweating profusely, you'll forget all about your daily stresses. The high-intensity nature of CrossFit and the competitive atmosphere make it impossible to focus on anything other than the workout at hand.

But CrossFit isn't just good for your mental health, it's also great for your physical well-being. It's a full-body workout that will push you to your limits and help you achieve new ones. Plus, the sense of community and belonging that comes with being part of the CrossFit scene is unmatched.

And let's not forget about the added bonus of having a strong and toned body. Who wouldn't want to look and feel their best while reducing their stress levels?

33. Kickboxing

Are you tired of feeling stressed out and overwhelmed? Want to find a new way to release all that pent up tension? Look no further than kickboxing! This high-energy workout is like a therapy session on steroids, allowing you to punch and kick away all your frustrations.

Imagine being able to let out all your anger on a punching bag, or getting a satisfying workout by kicking a heavy bag. It's like a form of stress-relieving therapy, where you can channel all your negative energy into something productive and physically demanding.

Kickboxing is not just about physical fitness, it's also a mental workout. It requires focus and discipline, which can help clear your mind and reduce stress. Imagine being able to leave all your worries behind as you focus on your movements and techniques.

And let's not forget the endorphins! The release of endorphins during a workout can improve your mood and reduce stress. So, not only will you be physically exhausted, but you'll also feel mentally refreshed and relaxed.

But kickboxing isn't just for the hardcore fitness enthusiasts. It's a workout that can be tailored to your fitness level, making it accessible to everyone. Whether you're a beginner or a pro, kickboxing can be a great stress-reliever for you.

So, why not give kickboxing a try? It's a fun and effective way to relieve stress and improve your overall well-being. And who knows, you might just discover a new hobby in the process.

Just a warning, your coworkers might get a bit nervous when you start punching and kicking your desk during a meeting, but trust us, it's worth it.

Time Management

When stress is high, it's like the boss of our brain, it takes over and starts making all the decisions for us. It tells us to put things off, to avoid the things that cause us stress, and before we know it, we're in a time management nightmare. It's like we're stuck in a never-ending game of whack-a-mole with our to-do list and no matter how many tasks we complete, more keep popping up.

We all know the feeling of having too much on our plate, the sensation of being overwhelmed and not knowing where to start. Stress amplifies this feeling and makes it hard to stay focused and prioritize our tasks. It's like trying to play a game of Tetris with one hand tied behind your back, you know what you need to do but the blocks keep falling faster and faster.

But it's not all doom and gloom, with a little bit of mindfulness, a dash of planning and a sprinkle of self-care, we can tame the stress-monster and take control of our time. We can learn to prioritize, to tackle the most important tasks first, and to not let the little things get in the way of the big picture.

34. Pomodoro

The Pomodoro Technique is a time management method that can help you increase productivity and reduce procrastination. The idea is simple: break your tasks into 25-minute intervals, called "Pomodoros," with a 5-minute break in between.

Here's how it works:

You start a timer for 25 minutes and begin working on a task.
Once the timer goes off, you take a 5-minute break.
After your break, you start another 25-minute Pomodoro and repeat the process.
Now, you might be thinking, "But wait, 25 minutes doesn't seem like enough time to get anything done!" And you know what? You're right. But here's the thing, when you're under a time constraint, you're more likely to focus on the task at hand and less likely to get sidetracked by the internet, social media, or the allure of your fridge. Plus, when you take a break every 25 minutes, you're giving your brain a chance to recharge and come back to the task with renewed energy.

The Pomodoro Technique is especially helpful for reducing daily stress because it allows you to break down big, overwhelming tasks into smaller, manageable chunks. Instead of feeling like you have to tackle a giant project all at once, you can break it down into several 25-minute Pomodoros.

And let's not forget the best part of the Pomodoro Technique: the 5-minute breaks! Use this time to stretch, grab a snack, check your phone, or even do a quick dance party. Trust me, these short breaks will not only refresh your mind but also put a smile on your face.

The Pomodoro Technique is a simple yet effective method to increase productivity and reduce procrastination. So, give it a try and experience the magic of 25-minute intervals. And remember, taking regular breaks is not procrastination, it's self-care. Happy Pomodoros!

35. Eisenhower Matrix

Ah, the Eisenhower Matrix. Named after the 34th President of the United States, Dwight D. Eisenhower, this handy little tool can help you prioritize your tasks and reduce daily stress. Here's how it works:

First, you take all of your tasks and put them into one of four categories:

Urgent and Important: These are tasks that need to be done ASAP and have a significant impact on your goals. Examples might include a deadline for a work project, a doctor's appointment, or a family emergency.

Important but Not Urgent: These are tasks that are important for achieving your goals, but don't have a pressing deadline. Examples might include exercise, learning a new skill, or building a relationship.

Urgent but Not Important: These are tasks that need to be done soon, but don't contribute much to your goals. Examples might include responding to a spam email, watching a cat video, or taking a pointless phone call.

Not Urgent or Important: These are tasks that don't need to be done soon and don't contribute much to your goals. Examples might include playing video games, watching TV, or browsing social media.

Now, I know what you're thinking: "But what about all the tasks that fall somewhere in between these categories? What about the gray area?" Well, my dear friend, that's where the beauty of the Eisenhower Matrix lies. It's not a black and white tool, but rather a way to help you see the bigger picture and make better decisions about how to spend your time.

So, here's the plan: tackle the tasks in category 1 first, then move on to category 2, then category 3, and finally, category 4. And if you're feeling particularly ambitious, you can even tackle multiple tasks at once (just make sure you're not spreading yourself too thin).

But wait, there's more! Not only can the Eisenhower Matrix help you prioritize your tasks, but it can also help you identify areas where you might be wasting time. For example, if you notice that a lot of your tasks fall into category 3 or 4, you might want to consider cutting back on those activities.

The Eisenhower Matrix is a great tool to help you prioritize your tasks and reduce daily stress, but remember that it's not a magic wand, and it's also important to have a good sense of humor about it all, because let's face it, sometimes the most important thing we can do for our mental health is to laugh at ourselves.

36. The 80/20 Rule

Ladies and gentlemen, let me introduce you to the magical world of the 80/20 rule, also known as the Pareto Principle. It's like a superhero power that can help you reduce your daily stress and increase your productivity at the same time.

Imagine you're a superhero, and you have a list of tasks to complete before the end of the day. Some tasks are small and easy to complete, like changing a light bulb or making a cup of coffee. Others are big and complex, like saving the world from an alien invasion or writing a novel. The 80/20 rule says that 80% of your results come from 20% of your efforts. In other words, you can get the same results by focusing on the 20% of tasks that will give you the most results.

For example, imagine you're a busy student, and you have a big exam coming up. You have a list of 100 things to study, but only 20 of them are essential for passing the exam. Instead of spending hours studying everything, you should focus on the 20% of things that will give you the most results. That way, you can pass the exam with less stress and more time to enjoy your life.

Now, let's say you're a business owner, and you have a lot of customers to deal with. 80% of your sales come from 20% of your customers. Instead of spending all your time trying to please everyone, you should focus on the 20% of customers that will give you the most results. That way, you can increase your sales and reduce your stress at the same time.

In conclusion, the 80/20 rule is a simple but powerful technique that can help you reduce your daily stress and increase your productivity. So next time you have a list of tasks to complete, remember to focus on the 20% of tasks that will give you the most results. And remember, with great power comes great responsibility, so use this power wisely and don't forget to have fun.

If you ever feel overwhelmed by the amount of things you have to do, just picture yourself as a superhero saving the world from an alien invasion and you'll feel better in no time.

37. Eat That Frog

Do you find yourself constantly putting off the most important tasks, only to feel guilty and frazzled later on? Well, it's time to hop to it and "Eat That Frog" with the technique made famous by author Brian Tracy.

The idea is simple: start your day by tackling the most important task first, the one you're most likely to procrastinate on. It's like eating a frog for breakfast - it may not be the most appetizing thing on the menu, but once it's done, the rest of your tasks will feel like a breeze.

For example, let's say you have a big presentation to give at work tomorrow, but you keep finding yourself scrolling through social media instead of preparing for it. Using the "Eat That Frog" technique, you would sit down first thing in the morning and work on your presentation until it's done. Not only will you feel a sense of accomplishment, but you'll also be more focused and productive for the rest of the day.

Another example, is you have to clean the house before the guests arrive tonight, but you're avoiding it like the plague. With the "Eat That Frog" technique, you'll tackle the cleaning first thing in the morning, and you'll be able to relax and enjoy your visitors with a clean house.

It's important to note that eating a frog is not easy, but it's not as bad as you think. It's like going to the gym. It's hard to get started but once you get going, you feel good about yourself.

By starting your day with the most important task, you'll not only reduce stress, but you'll also increase productivity and focus. So, don't be afraid to "Eat That Frog" and tackle those big tasks head-on. After all, what's the worst that could happen? You'll feel like a champion!

38. The Two-Minute Rule

The Two-Minute Rule is a simple yet powerful technique that can help you reduce daily stress and stay on top of your to-do list. The idea is simple: if a task takes less than two minutes to complete, do it right away. This might seem like a small thing, but trust me, it can make a big difference in the long run.

Let's say you're at work and you get an email from a colleague asking for a quick favor. Instead of putting it off and thinking "I'll do it later," use the Two-Minute Rule and just take care of it right away. It'll only take a couple of minutes, and you'll feel a sense of accomplishment and relief that it's done.

Or maybe you're at home and you notice that your kitchen is a mess. Instead of telling yourself "I'll clean it up later," grab a trash bag and spend two minutes putting things away. You'll be amazed at how much cleaner your kitchen will look and how much better you'll feel.

The Two-Minute Rule is also great for preventing small tasks from piling up and becoming overwhelming. We've all been there: we put off a small task thinking "it's not that important," only to have it grow into a much bigger task that's harder to tackle. By using the Two-Minute Rule, you can nip those small tasks in the bud before they become bigger problems.

So next time you're faced with a small task that you're tempted to put off, think about the Two-Minute Rule. It might just be the key to reducing your daily stress and staying on top of your to-do list. And remember, as the famous quote goes "Eat that frog", do the most challenging task first thing in the morning and the rest of the day will be a breeze.

Just imagine, you'll be able to enjoy your coffee break without the stress of pending tasks, it's like adding a pinch of sugar to your coffee, it just makes it taste better.

39. Don't Break the Chain

Well, I've got just the technique for you: The "Don't Break the Chain" Technique! It's simple, easy, and guaranteed to bring a smile to your face (and reduce that stress too, but let's not get too ahead of ourselves).

Here's how it works: grab a calendar and mark it with a big X every day you complete a task or achieve a goal. The goal is to keep the chain of X's going as long as possible, creating a visual representation of your progress. It's like a game of Tetris, but with your responsibilities. And who doesn't love a good game of Tetris?

But why stop there? Make it even more fun by using different colored pens for different types of tasks or goals. For example, use a red pen for work-related tasks, a blue pen for personal tasks, and a green pen for fitness goals. The possibilities are endless. Just make sure you have enough pens, otherwise, you'll be stuck with an unbroken chain of X's in one color, which might be a bit boring.

Now, I know what you might be thinking: "But what happens if I miss a day and break the chain?" Don't worry, it's not the end of the world. Just pick yourself up, dust yourself off and keep going. The point of this technique is not to be perfect, but to make progress and have fun while doing it.

So, go ahead and give it a try. I guarantee you'll feel a sense of accomplishment and satisfaction every time you see that chain of X's growing longer and longer. It's like a hug, but for your calendar. So, go forth and conquer your daily tasks and goals, and don't break that chain!

40. Three Things

Do you find yourself constantly getting sidetracked and never quite completing everything you set out to do? Well, I have just the technique for you: The "Three Things" Technique.

It's pretty simple: every morning, before you start your day, write down three things you want to accomplish. These should be the most important tasks that you need to get done that day. Then, throughout the day, focus all your energy on completing these three things.

I know, you're probably thinking "But wait, what about all the other things on my to-do list? Won't I just be ignoring them?" Well, here's the thing: we all have a limited amount of focus and energy each day. By focusing on just three things, you'll be able to give each task your full attention and complete them more efficiently. Plus, by crossing off those three most important tasks, you'll feel a sense of accomplishment that'll motivate you to tackle the rest of your to-do list.

Let me give you an example: say you're a student and you have a big exam coming up. Your three things for the day could be: 1) Study for two hours, 2) Take practice test, 3) Review flashcards. By focusing on these three things, you'll be able to make the most of your study time and feel confident going into the exam.

Or maybe you're a working professional and your three things for the day are: 1) Finish that report, 2) Have a meeting with a client, 3) Send an email follow-up. By focusing on these three things, you'll be able to get that report done, have a productive meeting, and keep the ball rolling with the client.

It's like a superhero suit that gives you the power of focus and discipline, with a hint of humor and motivation. So next time you're feeling overwhelmed and sidetracked, give the "Three Things" Technique a try. Trust me, it'll make your life easier.

41. Time Blocking

Do you find yourself constantly overbooking yourself and then scrambling to get everything done? Well, my friend, it's time to try out the "Time Blocking" Technique.

This technique involves setting aside specific time slots in your schedule for different tasks and activities. For example, let's say you want to spend an hour each day working on your side hustle. You would block out that hour in your calendar and dedicate it solely to working on your side hustle.

Not only does this technique help keep you on track, but it also prevents overbooking yourself. Let's say you have a big project due at work and you know it's going to take a good chunk of your time. By blocking out specific time slots for that project, you'll be able to see exactly when you have available time for other things.

But here's the thing, we all know it's easy to get sidetracked. You might be tempted to check your social media, catch up on the latest memes or watch that cute cat video that just poped on youtube, but with time blocking you'll be able to stay focused and get more done in less time.

To make the most of this technique, try using a calendar app or a planner to schedule your time blocks. And don't be afraid to get creative with your time blocks! You could block out 30 minutes in the morning for a yoga session, or an hour in the evening for a date night with yourself.

And remember, time blocking isn't just for work and productivity. It's also a great way to make sure you're taking care of yourself and making time for the things that matter most to you.

So, give it a try and see how it can help reduce your daily stress and make you feel more in control of your time. And remember, the key to success with time blocking is consistency, so don't be too hard on yourself if you slip up every now and then. You're human, not a robot (yet).

42. "One-Touch"

This technique is all about handling each task or piece of information only once. That's right, no more procrastination, no more putting things off for later, and no more feeling overwhelmed.

For example, let's say you get an email from your boss asking for a report on the company's sales for the past quarter. Instead of just reading the email and leaving it in your inbox for later, you can use the "One-Touch" Technique by immediately replying to the email with a confirmation of receipt, creating a calendar reminder for yourself to work on the report, and then finally, completing the report and sending it off to your boss.

Another example, let's say you're at home and you see a pile of laundry that needs to be done. Instead of just looking at it and thinking "I'll do it later", you can use the "One-Touch" Technique by sorting the laundry by color, starting a load of whites, and then folding the clothes that are already dry.

By following the "One-Touch" Technique, you'll find that things will be less overwhelming, and you'll have more time to enjoy the important things in life like Netflix and chill or playing video games. And if you're still feeling stressed, just remember, "One-Touch" is not just a technique, it's a lifestyle choice. So go out there and conquer your to-do list like a boss.

43. Five-Minute Rule

Welcome to the world of the "Five-Minute Rule"! This simple yet effective technique is perfect for anyone looking to reduce daily stress and conquer procrastination. The idea is simple: give yourself five minutes to complete a task that you're procrastinating on. If you're not done in five minutes, give yourself five more minutes and so on, until the task is completed.

Here's an example of how the Five-Minute Rule can work in real life: imagine you're trying to organize your closet, but you're feeling overwhelmed and just can't seem to get started. You know that once you get started, you'll probably enjoy the process, but you're just not feeling it right now. Instead of giving up and succumbing to the dreaded "I'll do it later" mentality, you can use the Five-Minute Rule to help you get started.

First, set a timer for five minutes and commit to working on your closet for that amount of time. Once the timer starts, you'll be surprised at how quickly five minutes can fly by! Chances are, you'll be making progress and finding it hard to stop when the timer goes off. That's when you can give yourself five more minutes and so on, until the task is completed.

Another example where the Five-Minute Rule could be helpful is when you're trying to write an essay, but you're feeling stuck and unable to focus. You can use the Five-Minute Rule to help you get started. Set a timer for five minutes and commit to writing for that amount of time. Once the timer starts, you'll be surprised at how quickly you'll be able to focus and put words on paper.

The best part about the Five-Minute Rule is that it's so simple, anyone can do it! So the next time you're feeling overwhelmed or procrastinating on a task, give the Five-Minute Rule a try. Just remember, five minutes is all it takes to get started and conquer procrastination. And don't forget, a little bit of humour never hurts, so don't be afraid to make it fun!

44. To-Don't List

We all have those days where we feel like we have a never-ending list of things to do and not enough time to do them. And let's be even more real, most of us have a love-hate relationship with our to-do lists. We love the feeling of crossing off tasks and the sense of accomplishment it brings, but we also hate the stress and pressure that comes with having a mile-long list. So, what if I told you there was a way to reduce that stress and pressure while still being productive? Enter: the "To-Don't" list.

Instead of making a list of things you need to do, make a list of things you should not do. These can be things that are not important, things that can wait, or even things that you know will add unnecessary stress to your day. For example, instead of writing "answer all emails" on your to-do list, write "don't check email before 10am." This not only sets boundaries for yourself, but it also allows you to prioritize the tasks that truly need to be done.

Another great thing about the "To-Don't" list is that it allows you to be more mindful of your time. Instead of mindlessly scrolling through social media during your lunch break, you can write "don't check social media during lunch" on your list. This not only helps you to be more present in the moment, but it also allows you to be more productive with the time you do have.

And let's not forget the added bonus of a little bit of humor. For example, instead of writing "don't procrastinate," write "don't put off until tomorrow what you can do the day after tomorrow." It's a little reminder to not take things too seriously and to have a little bit of fun with it.

So, the next time you're feeling overwhelmed and stressed by your to-do list, try switching things up and making a "To-Don't" list. Not only will it help you to prioritize and be more mindful of your time, but it also adds a touch of humor to an otherwise mundane task.

45. Pairing

The concept is simple: pair a task you don't want to do with a task you do want to do. For example, let's say you're a huge fan of the show "Stranger Things" (who isn't, am I right?), but you hate cleaning your house. Instead of dreading the thought of cleaning, why not make it a little more bearable by watching an episode of "Stranger Things" while you tidy up?

Or maybe you're a podcast fanatic, but you can't stand doing the dishes. Well, why not put on your favorite podcast and wash those dishes with a smile on your face?

The key to the "Pairing" Technique is to find something you enjoy and use it as a reward for completing a task you don't like. It's like the adult version of "If you eat your vegetables, you can have dessert."

But it's not just about using TV shows and podcasts as rewards. You can pair any task you don't want to do with something you enjoy. For example, if you love to read but hate doing laundry, why not curl up with a good book while you fold your clothes?

By using the "Pairing" Technique, not only will you be getting things done, but you'll also be reducing your stress levels. So, next time you're faced with a task you don't want to do, just think to yourself "What's my reward going to be?" and before you know it, you'll have a clean house, a full laundry basket and a happy you.

46. Three-Minute Breather

Now, I know what you're thinking: "Three minutes? That's it? That's not enough time to do anything!" But trust me, my dear friends, this little break can work wonders for your productivity and overall well-being.

The technique is simple: every hour, take a three-minute break to breathe deeply, stretch, and refocus. That's it! No need to go for a run or meditate for an hour (although those things are great too). Just a quick break to give your mind and body a little bit of TLC.

Now, I know what some of you might be thinking: "But I don't have time for a break! I have work to do!" And to that, I say: my dear friend, you are exactly the person who needs this technique the most. Taking a quick break every hour can actually increase your productivity in the long run. By giving your brain a little rest, you'll be able to tackle your work with renewed focus and energy.

And let's be real, it's not just your productivity that will benefit from this technique. Your overall well-being will improve as well. Taking a few minutes to breathe deeply and stretch can help to relieve stress, prevent burnout and improve your overall mood.

Now, I know that some of you might be thinking: "But I'm not a flexible person, I can't do stretches" Don't worry, you don't have to do yoga poses, a simple stretch on your neck and back will do the trick.

So, there you have it, folks. The Three-Minute Breather Technique: a quick, easy, and effective way to reduce stress and increase productivity. Remember, take a break every hour and breathe deeply, stretch, and refocus. Trust me, your mind and body will thank you for it.

Let's all take a deep breath together and stretch our legs, it's break time!

47. Two-Minute Break

Well, have no fear, because the "Two-Minute Break" technique is here to save the day! This simple, yet effective method involves taking a two-minute break every 20 minutes to breathe deeply, stretch, and refocus. It's like hitting the reset button on your brain, so you can tackle your tasks with renewed energy and focus.

Think of it like a mini vacation for your mind, without having to leave your desk or spend a dime. Just set a timer for 20 minutes and work on your task, and when it goes off, take a two-minute break. During this time, you can do some deep breathing exercises, stretch your legs, or even just stand up and walk around a bit. This will help increase blood flow and oxygen to your brain, and get you out of that sedentary position.

Now you might be thinking, "But two minutes is so short, how could it possibly make a difference?" Well, my friend, let me tell you, those two minutes can make all the difference in the world. It's like taking a sip of water when you're thirsty, or taking a bite of a cookie when you're craving something sweet. It might not solve all your problems, but it sure does make them feel a little more manageable.

Let me give you an example. Imagine you've been staring at a spreadsheet for hours, and your brain is starting to feel like mush. You're having trouble focusing, and your eyes are starting to cross. But wait, your timer goes off, signaling it's time for a two-minute break. You take a deep breath, stand up and stretch your legs, and then refocus on your task. And just like that, you're back in the game. Your brain feels clearer, and you're able to tackle that spreadsheet with renewed vigor.

So, if you're looking to reduce daily stress and increase productivity, give the "Two-Minute Break" technique a try. It's like a little vacation for your brain, without having to leave your desk or spend a dime. And who knows, you might even find yourself looking forward to your next break. Just don't get too excited and start doing somersaults in the office, that might not go over too well.

48. Set a Time Limit

This technique is simple yet effective. All you have to do is set a time limit for each task on your to-do list and make sure to stick to it. For example, if you have to write a report for work, set a time limit of two hours for it. Once that two hours is up, take a break and move on to the next task.

This may seem counterintuitive, as you may think that you need more time to complete a task, but trust me, the time limit will actually help you to focus and be more productive. It's like having a personal trainer for your brain, pushing you to work harder and faster.

Not only will this technique help you to focus and be more productive, but it will also help to prevent you from getting bogged down and losing focus. We've all been there, staring at a computer screen for hours on end, feeling like our brains are turning to mush. With the "Set a Time Limit" technique, you'll be able to take frequent breaks, which will help to refresh your mind and give you the energy you need to tackle the next task.

And the best part? You'll be able to cross off items on your to-do list in no time, leaving you with a sense of accomplishment and a lot less stress. Imagine being able to tell your boss "I finished that report you needed in 2 hours" and watch as their jaw drops in amazement

So, the next time you're feeling overwhelmed by your to-do list, try out the "Set a Time Limit" technique. It's like having a personal superhero, who will help you to focus, be productive and reduce stress. With this technique, you'll be able to conquer your to-do list in no time and have plenty of time for the important things in life, like binge-watching your favorite show or having a nap.

49. "5-5-5"

The "5-5-5" technique is easy to follow and can be done anywhere, whether you're working from home or in an office. All you need to do is take five deep breaths, five minutes to stretch or move your body, and five minutes to refocus and plan your next task.

Let's break it down step by step. First, take five deep breaths. This might sound silly, but deep breathing can do wonders for your mental and physical well-being. It helps to oxygenate your brain and reduce stress levels. Plus, it's a quick and easy way to clear your head and get rid of the "brain fog" that can often accompany long periods of sitting.

Next, take five minutes to stretch or move your body. This can be anything from a quick yoga flow to a simple walk around the block. The key is to get up and move your body. Sitting for long periods of time can lead to stiffness and muscle tension, so it's important to take a break and give your body a little TLC. Plus, it's a great way to get your blood flowing and boost your energy levels.

Finally, take five minutes to refocus and plan your next task. This is the perfect time to jot down any thoughts or ideas that have been swirling around in your head, or to simply take a moment to clear your mind. It's also a great opportunity to plan your next steps and set some goals for the rest of the day.

50. Pomodoro-Eisenhower

The Pomodoro Technique is a time management method that involves breaking your work into 25-minute intervals, or "pomodoros", with short breaks in between. The Eisenhower Matrix is a tool for prioritizing tasks based on their urgency and importance. By combining these two methods, you'll be able to tackle your tasks with laser-like focus and efficiency.

Here's how it works: First, take a look at your to-do list and decide which tasks are the most urgent and important. Put those in the "do first" category. Next, look at the tasks that are important but not as urgent. Put those in the "schedule" category. Finally, look at the tasks that are neither urgent nor important. Put those in the "delegate or eliminate" category.

Now, take the tasks in the "do first" category and break them down into 25-minute intervals. Set a timer and focus on that task for 25 minutes. Once the timer goes off, take a short break (5 minutes is good). Then, start the next 25-minute interval. Repeat this process until the task is finished.

Now, for the tasks in the "schedule" category, you'll want to schedule them for a specific time during the day. And for the tasks in the "delegate or eliminate" category, well, you know what to do.

The beauty of this technique is that it allows you to focus on one task at a time, without the distractions of other tasks looming in the back of your mind. And by prioritizing your tasks based on their urgency and importance, you'll be able to tackle the most important things first and not waste time on things that don't matter.

51. Two-Minute Review

The idea behind this technique is simple: every two minutes, take a quick break and review your progress and tasks. This may sound crazy at first, but trust me, it's a game changer. By taking these mini breaks, you'll be able to keep track of what you've done, what still needs to be done, and make any necessary adjustments.

For example, let's say you're working on a big project at work. Instead of getting lost in the work and losing track of time, you set a timer for two minutes. When the timer goes off, you quickly review what you've done, make sure you're on track, and maybe even make a to-do list for the next two minutes. This way, you're constantly aware of your progress and can make any necessary adjustments to stay on schedule.

But the Two-Minute Review Technique isn't just for work. It can be applied to anything in your life. Let's say you're trying to lose weight and you're on a diet. Every two minutes, you can review what you've eaten, make sure you're sticking to your diet plan, and adjust accordingly. Or maybe you're trying to quit smoking. Every two minutes, you can review how many cigarettes you've had, and make a plan to decrease that number.

The possibilities are endless, and the best part is it's super easy to implement. All you need is a timer and a willingness to take control of your time and stress levels. So, don't let stress be the boss of you, be the boss of your stress with the Two-Minute Review Technique.

52. Three-Step Rule

The Three-Step Rule is all about breaking down tasks into manageable steps and ensuring that nothing is missed. And the best part is, it's so easy to use. Here's how it works:

Create a plan: Before you start any task, take a moment to think about what you need to do and how you're going to do it. Write down a list of steps and make sure you understand what needs to be done. It's like having a roadmap for your task, and it will save you a lot of stress and confusion later on.

Execute it: Now that you have a plan, it's time to put it into action. This is where the real work happens. Follow the steps you've written down, and don't be afraid to make adjustments as you go along. Remember, your plan is just a guide, not a rulebook.

Review it: Once you've finished your task, take a moment to reflect on what you've done. Did you miss anything? Is there anything you could have done better? Use this information to improve your plan for next time. And give yourself a pat on the back for a job well done!

Let me give you an example of how this technique works in practice. Let's say you're planning a party. First, you create a plan and write down a list of things you need to do, like sending out invitations, buying decorations, and making a menu. Next, you execute your plan by sending out the invitations, buying the decorations, and making the menu. Finally, you review your plan and see if there's anything you missed or anything you could have done better. And voila! You've just thrown an amazing party without any stress.

But don't just take my word for it, try it out for yourself. I promise you, The Three-Step Rule is like having a personal stress-busting superhero on your side. And honestly, who doesn't want a superhero in their life? So give it a try and watch your stress levels drop faster than a superhero saving a cat stuck in a tree.

53. The Two-List Technique

First, grab a piece of paper (or open a new note on your phone) and make two columns. Label the first column "Short-Term Goals" and the second column "Long-Term Goals". Now, start brainstorming all the things you want to accomplish, both in the short-term and long-term.

For your short-term goals, think about the tasks and responsibilities that need to be done in the next week or two. These could include things like finishing a project at work, cleaning the house, or going to the gym. These are the "must-dos" that need to be completed in order to keep your life running smoothly.

On the other hand, your long-term goals are the big dreams and aspirations you have for yourself. These could include things like buying a house, starting your own business, or traveling to a new country. These are the things that will bring you true fulfillment and happiness in the long run.

The beauty of the Two-List Technique is that it helps you keep your focus on both the big picture and the small details. By writing down your long-term goals, you'll be reminded of what you're working towards and why it's important. And by completing your short-term goals, you'll be making progress towards achieving those long-term goals.

Plus, it's always a good feeling to cross something off a list, right? So go ahead, give the Two-List Technique a try and reduce your daily stress. And remember, don't forget to add a few fun things to your lists too, like "Watch a comedy special" or "Make a homemade pizza" to bring some humour and balance in your life.

With the Two-List Technique, you'll be able to tackle your to-do list with a clear mind and a sense of purpose. Happy goal-setting!

Social Support

Social support is one of the most powerful tools we have for managing stress and leading a happy, fulfilled life.

We all know that feeling of stress creeping up on us, like a dark cloud looming overhead. It's like the universe is conspiring against us and we're stuck in a never-ending cycle of negative thoughts and worries. But here's the thing, we don't have to face stress alone. In fact, it's often the support of our loved ones that can help us weather the storm.

Think of social support as a life jacket in the rough seas of stress. It's that extra bit of buoyancy that keeps us from going under. It's the hand that pulls us back to safety when we're about to drown in our worries. Without social support, stress can feel like a lonely, never-ending battle. But with it, we can face our fears head-on and come out on top.

For example, imagine you're having a bad day at work, and you come home to find your partner has made you your favorite dinner and has a warm hug waiting for you. Or, you're feeling overwhelmed by a big project, and a friend offers to help you break it down into manageable tasks. Or, you're feeling down and a family member makes you laugh with a silly joke. These small acts of kindness and support can make all the difference in the world when it comes to managing stress.

Social support comes in many forms, from a simple text message from a friend, to a night out with the girls, to a heart-to-heart with your mom. It doesn't matter if it's a significant other, a best friend, a family member, or a therapist, what matters is that you have someone you can turn to when things get tough. And let's be real, things will get tough. That's just life. But with social

77

support, we can face those tough times head-on and come out stronger on the other side.

54. Join a club or group that aligns with your interests

One great way to alleviate stress is by surrounding yourself with people who share similar interests as you. Joining a club or group that aligns with your interests can not only provide you with a sense of community, but it can also help you build deeper connections.

For example, if hiking is your thing, why not join a hiking club? Not only will you get to explore beautiful trails and scenery, but you'll also get to bond with fellow nature enthusiasts. And if knitting is more your speed, a knitting group is the perfect way to relax, unwind, and create something beautiful, all while chatting with like-minded individuals.

And let's not forget about the added bonus of a little friendly competition. Whether it's a hiking club's weekly hike challenge or a knitting group's sweater-making contest, these friendly competitions can be a great way to push yourself out of your comfort zone and achieve new goals.

But it's not just about the activities themselves, it's also about the people. Joining a club or group can give you a sense of belonging and camaraderie that can be hard to find in everyday life. It's always fun to have a group of people to share in your passions, and to make inside jokes with

So, whether you're into hiking, knitting, or anything in between, joining a club or group is a great way to reduce stress and build deeper connections. And who knows, you might even discover a new hobby or passion along the way. So go forth, and join a club today, and let the good times roll!

55. Volunteer in your community

Volunteering in your community is a win-win situation. Not only are you making a difference in the lives of others, but you're also getting a dose of good karma and a feel-good boost for yourself. And who doesn't love a good feel-good story at the end of the day? It's like a warm hug from the universe.

Plus, volunteering is a great way to meet new people and build connections. Think of it as a social mixer with a purpose. You never know who you might meet while serving meals at a soup kitchen or helping out at a local animal shelter. You could make a new friend, a business connection, or even a romantic partner. It's like speed dating, but with more altruism and less awkward silences.

And the best part is, there are so many ways to volunteer in your community. Whether you have an hour to spare or a whole day, there's a volunteer opportunity that's perfect for you. Here are a few examples:

If you're a morning person, consider volunteering at a local food bank or pantry. You'll get to start your day feeling like a superhero for helping feed those in need.

If you're a dog lover, why not spend some time at your local animal shelter? You'll get to hang out with some adorable furry friends and maybe even help them find their forever home.

If you're a green thumb, consider volunteering at a community garden. Not only will you be helping grow fresh produce for those in need, but you'll also get to enjoy some fresh air and sunshine.

If you're a bookworm, consider volunteering at a local library. You'll get to help others find their next great read and maybe even discover a few new favorites yourself.

So, don't just sit there stressing out about your to-do list. Get out there and make a difference in your community. Not only will you feel good about yourself, but you'll also have some great stories to share with your friends and family. And who knows, you might just meet some new friends and build some valuable connections along the way. So, go forth and volunteer, my friends. Your community, and your stress levels, will thank you.

56. Attend networking events

Networking events are the perfect opportunity to reduce daily stress and build connections. Not only do they allow you to meet new people, but they also offer a chance to expand your professional or social circle.

One of the best things about networking events is that they come in all shapes and sizes. Whether it's a professional conference, a social mixer, or a community event, there's something for everyone. And the best part? You don't have to be an extrovert to enjoy them. Even introverts can benefit from networking events. They're a great way to practice socializing in a low-pressure environment.

But before you head out to your next networking event, there are a few things you should keep in mind. First and foremost, don't forget to bring your business cards. It's always a good idea to have them on hand in case you meet someone who may be interested in your services or products. And don't worry if you run out, because you never know when you'll meet someone who will ask you for one, so it's better to be safe than sorry.

Another important tip is to remember to bring a smile. Yes, it sounds simple, but it's one of the most important things you can do when networking. A smile is a universal sign of friendliness and approachability. It's also a great way to break the ice and make a good first impression.

Networking events are also a great opportunity to have some fun and let loose. After all, who says networking has to be all business? Make sure to enjoy yourself, and don't be afraid to let your personality shine through. After all, people want to do business with people they like, so let your sense of humour come through.

57. Take a class or workshop

Now, I know what you're thinking - " I'm not a class kind of person." But hear me out - you don't have to go back to college and get a degree in something. Just think about something you've always been curious about and sign up for a class or workshop in that topic. It could be something as simple as a cooking class, where you learn how to make the perfect risotto and meet some foodies in the process. Or maybe a photography workshop, where you can finally figure out what all those buttons on your camera do, and make some new friends with a shared interest in capturing the perfect shot.

But it's not just about meeting new people and having a good time, taking a class or workshop also has some serious benefits. For one, it's a great way to reduce daily stress. When you're learning something new, your brain is forced to focus on the task at hand and not dwelling on the past or worrying about the future. Plus, you'll be expanding your skillset, which is always a plus. Who knows, that cooking class might lead to a new hobby or even a career change. We could all use a little more variety in our lives.

So, don't be afraid to step out of your comfort zone and try something new. You never know, it might just be the change you needed. And if nothing else, you'll have a few new recipes or Instagram-worthy photos to show for it.

58. Start a book club or movie club

Starting a book club or movie club is a fantastic way to bond with friends and family over shared interests, and have some fun at the same time. Not only that, but it's also an excellent way to reduce daily stress. Here's how it works:

First, gather a group of like-minded individuals who are interested in discussing books or movies. This could be friends, family, or even strangers you meet online. Once you have your group, decide on a regular meeting day and time that works for everyone.

Next, choose a book or movie to discuss each month. You could take turns selecting the title, or you could use a randomizer to keep things interesting. The important thing is to make sure everyone has enough time to read or watch the title before the meeting.

Then, on the day of the meeting, gather together and discuss the book or movie. This is where the fun begins! Share your thoughts and opinions, and listen to others as they share their perspectives. You might be surprised by how much you learn from each other.

One of the best things about a book or movie club is that it gives you an excuse to take a break from the stresses of everyday life. Rather than focusing on work, family, or other responsibilities, you can relax and enjoy the company of others. And who knows, you might even discover a new favorite book or movie!

But don't just take my word for it, give it a try! Start a book club or movie club with your friends and family, and see for yourself how much fun it can be. And if you're feeling really adventurous, why not start a book AND movie club? That way, you'll have twice the fun and twice the opportunities to bond with your loved ones.

59. Attend religious or spiritual gatherings

Attending religious or spiritual gatherings can be a great way to reduce daily stress and build a sense of belonging. Whether you're a devout believer or simply seeking a sense of community, there are many benefits to joining a church, temple, or other religious community.

For starters, religious and spiritual gatherings often provide a sense of structure and routine. This can be especially helpful for those who may be feeling overwhelmed by the chaos of everyday life. By committing to attend regular services or meetings, you can create a sense of stability and predictability that can help to ease stress and anxiety.

Another benefit of religious or spiritual gatherings is the sense of belonging that they can provide. Joining a community of like-minded individuals can be incredibly empowering, as it allows you to connect with others who share your values and beliefs. This can be especially helpful for those who may be feeling lonely or isolated, as it can provide a sense of support and camaraderie.

Of course, let's not forget about the spiritual aspect of religious gatherings. Many people find comfort in prayer and meditation, and find that these practices help them to feel more connected to something greater than themselves. This can be a powerful way to reduce stress and find inner peace.

And if you're worried about getting bored, just remember that you can always try to spot the person who always falls asleep during the sermon. Or if you're not a fan of singing, just hum along and pretend you know the words. Trust me, it's a great stress-reliever.

60. Attend a concert, play or sports event

Going to a concert, play, or sports event is the perfect way to forget about your daily stress and have some fun. Not only will you get to see your favorite band or team in action, but you'll also be surrounded by people who share your interests. It's a great opportunity to connect with like-minded individuals and maybe even make some new friends.

For example, let's say you're a huge fan of the band "The Beatles." Imagine the excitement you would feel as you make your way to a concert venue to see a tribute band perform all of your favorite songs. The energy in the room is electric as the band takes the stage and starts playing "Twist and Shout." The crowd is singing and dancing along, and for a moment, all of your troubles disappear. You're lost in the music and having the time of your life.

Or maybe you're a die-hard basketball fan and you have tickets to see your favorite team play. The thrill of being in the arena as your team takes the court is something that can't be matched. As the game heats up and the tension builds, you're on the edge of your seat cheering and shouting encouragement to your team. And when they win, the feeling of pure elation is indescribable.

Even if you're not a huge fan of any particular team or band, going to a sports event or concert is still a great way to have a good time. The atmosphere is always lively, and you never know who you might meet. You might strike up a conversation with the person sitting next to you and discover that you have a lot in common. Who knows? They might even become your new best friend.

61. Take a trip with friends or family

Whether it's a quick weekend getaway or a longer vacation, traveling with loved ones is the ultimate stress-buster. Not only will you get to explore new places and make unforgettable memories, but you'll also get to bond and build deeper connections with the people you care about most.

Just imagine the laughs you'll have as you navigate a new city together, the inside jokes you'll create, and the memories you'll make. Not to mention, the group photos you'll have to show off to all your envious friends back home.

And let's not forget about the added bonus of not having to make any decisions. No more deciding what to eat, what to do, or where to go. Just sit back, relax, and let the group make all the choices for you. It's like a mini-vacation from decision making.

Plus, traveling with a group means that you'll have built-in entertainment. I mean, have you ever traveled with a group of friends and NOT had a good time? It's pretty much impossible. Plus, you'll have people to share the cost with, making it a budget-friendly option.

So, what are you waiting for? Start planning that trip with your loved ones and get ready to make some unforgettable memories, bond with your favorite people and most importantly, reduce your daily stress. Trust me, your mind, body and soul will thank you for it.

62. Attend social events

I know, I know, you're probably thinking "I just want to Netflix and chill" and I totally get that. But hear me out. Social events, whether it's a party, barbecue, or potluck dinner, are great opportunities to connect with friends and family, and what's more stress-relieving than a good old fashioned gossip session with your squad?

Let's start with parties. Now, I know what you're thinking, "Parties are loud and overwhelming and I just want to hide in the corner with a drink." And I get that, believe me. But have you ever noticed how much more relaxed and carefree you feel after a good dance sesh with your besties? Plus, with the added bonus of free drinks and snacks, what's not to love?

Next up, barbecues. Now, I know the thought of standing around a hot grill in the summer heat doesn't sound like the most stress-relieving activity, but think about the payoff. The smell of burgers and hot dogs grilling, the sound of laughter and good conversation, and let's not forget, the taste of that perfectly cooked burger. Plus, you can always grab a cold drink and sneak away for a quick stress-relieving game of cornhole.

And finally, potluck dinners. Now, I know some of you may be thinking "I'm not a great cook, I don't want to bring something that's going to be the laughing stock of the party." But that's the beauty of potlucks, everyone brings something, so even if your dish isn't the best, it's just one of many. Plus, it's always fun to see what creative dishes your friends and family come up with.

63. Connect with friends and family on social network

Social media can be a great way to stay in touch with loved ones, even if they live far away. Imagine being able to see your niece's first steps, or your cousin's graduation, all from the comfort of your own home. No more waiting for the yearly family reunion or that one phone call a month, you can now have a front-row seat to all the important moments in your loved ones' lives.

But it's not just about catching up on big events, social media also allows for the small, everyday moments to be shared. Imagine being able to send a quick "good morning" message to your sister who lives on the other side of the country, or sending a "thinking of you" meme to your best friend who's going through a tough time. These little gestures can make a big difference in maintaining relationships and feeling connected to those we care about.

And let's not forget the added bonus of being able to make new friends on social media. You never know, that random person you added on Instagram because of their cute dog may just turn out to be your new BFF. So, don't be afraid to branch out and connect with new people, it's not just for the college days.

But social media can also be a source of stress. The constant stream of notifications, the pressure to present a perfect life, and the constant comparison can be overwhelming. So, my advice, use social media as a tool to connect with loved ones, not as a source of stress. And remember, the best way to reduce daily stress is to log off, and go have a good old-fashioned phone call with a friend or family member. Nothing beats hearing their voice and having a good laugh together.

64. Seek out a mentor

Let me tell you, finding a mentor is like finding a pot of gold at the end of a rainbow. Except, you know, way more valuable. Not only do they provide guidance and support, but they also serve as a sounding board for your ideas. And who doesn't need a little extra support and guidance in their life? Especially when it comes to reducing daily stress.

Here's a little story to illustrate my point. Imagine you're a young, ambitious unicorn. You've got big dreams and big ideas, but you're also feeling a little lost and stressed out. You're trying to navigate the big, wide world, and it can be overwhelming. That's when you meet an older, wiser unicorn. This mentor takes you under their wing and shows you the ropes. They teach you how to fly, how to use your magical powers, and how to avoid those pesky dragons. Without them, you'd be floundering, but with their guidance, you're able to soar.

In a similar way, a mentor in your personal or professional life can help you navigate the tricky waters of adulting. They can provide you with valuable advice and experience, and help you avoid the mistakes they've made in the past. They can help you develop your skills and set you on the path to success.

But here's the thing, finding a mentor can be tricky. It's not like they're just hanging out at the local Starbucks, waiting to be discovered. You've got to put yourself out there and actively seek out a mentor. You can start by networking and connecting with people in your industry. Attend events, join professional organizations, and don't be afraid to reach out to people you admire. And if you can't find a mentor in person, there are plenty of online resources and communities where you can connect with experienced professionals.

Don't be like that poor little unicorn, floundering in the world without a mentor. Take control of your stress and seek out someone who can guide and support you on your journey. And remember, a little bit of humor can go a long way in reducing stress, so don't be afraid to have fun and make a few jokes along the way.

65. Join a support group

Sometimes the best way to reduce stress is to connect with others who are going through similar experiences. And that's where support groups come in.

Now, I know what you might be thinking. "I don't want to sit in a circle and talk about my feelings with a bunch of strangers." And honestly, that's a fair point. But let me tell you, support groups are not just for people going through therapy or dealing with mental health issues. They can be for anyone looking to find a sense of community and connection.

For example, let's say you're a new parent and you're feeling overwhelmed with the responsibilities of taking care of a tiny human. Joining a parenting support group can provide a safe space for you to connect with other new parents and share tips, tricks, and most importantly, vent about the struggles of parenthood. You might even make some new friends who you can commiserate with over a glass of wine (or a cup of coffee, depending on the time of day).

Or maybe you're a recent college graduate and you're struggling to adjust to the "real world". Joining a young adult support group can provide a space for you to connect with others who are going through similar struggles and find support and encouragement as you navigate this new chapter in your life.

There's even support groups for people who just love to knit! Yes, you heard me right, a knitting support group! where you can share your knitting projects, ask for advice on patterns, and maybe even make some new friends.

The point is, support groups can be for anyone looking to find a sense of community and connection. So, if you're feeling stressed out and in need of some support, why not give it a try? Who knows, you might just find your tribe.

P.S. Don't forget to bring your knitting needles if you decide to join the knitting support group

66. Take a fitness class

Whether you're into yoga, Pilates, or spinning, there's a class out there that's perfect for you. Not only will you get a great workout, but you'll also have the opportunity to meet new people, build connections, and improve your physical and mental health all at the same time.

For example, imagine you're feeling stressed out from work and decide to take a yoga class. Not only will you get to stretch out those tight muscles and breathe deeply, but you'll also be surrounded by a supportive community of yogis who are all working towards the same goal: feeling better. Plus, with all the "Om"ing and "Namaste"ing going on, you're bound to get a few laughs in, too.

Or maybe you're feeling a little down and decide to take a Pilates class. Not only will you get to strengthen your core and improve your posture, but you'll also get to bond with your fellow Pilates enthusiasts over shared struggles to balance on one leg while holding a giant rubber band. Trust me, it's a bonding experience like no other.

And if you're feeling like you need to let off some steam, a spinning class might be just the thing. Not only will you get an intense cardio workout, but you'll also get to channel your inner rockstar as you pedal to the beat of the music. There's nothing like screaming "I will survive!" at the top of your lungs to a room full of strangers to make you feel like you can conquer the world.

67. Meet your neighbors

One of the simplest and most effective ways to reduce stress and build a sense of belonging is to get to know your neighbors.

There are many ways to meet your neighbors, whether it's through a neighborhood association, community garden, or just chatting over the fence. For example, if you're a green thumb, you might want to join a community garden. Not only will you get to spend some time outdoors and enjoy the fruits of your labor, but you'll also get to know other people who are passionate about gardening. Plus, if you're ever in need of a tomato or some basil, you know who to ask!

Another way to meet your neighbors is by joining a neighborhood association. Many neighborhoods have these groups, which typically meet regularly to discuss issues and plan events. Joining one of these groups is a great way to stay informed about what's going on in your neighborhood and to get to know your neighbors. Plus, you'll have a say in how your community is run, which can be very empowering.

Finally, don't underestimate the power of a simple chat over the fence. Sometimes, all it takes to start building a sense of community is to strike up a conversation with the person next door. Just be sure to approach it with a sense of humor and don't forget to bring a cup of sugar if you're going to borrow some.

Getting to know your neighbors is a simple but powerful way to reduce stress and build a sense of community. So, don't be shy, step out of your comfort zone, and start chatting with your neighbors today!

68. Start a hobby

Starting a hobby is a fantastic way to reduce daily stress and build connections with like-minded individuals. Whether it's knitting, gardening, or painting, there are countless options to choose from.

For example, if you're feeling a little crafty, why not try knitting? Not only is it a relaxing and meditative activity, but you'll also end up with a cozy scarf or sweater at the end of it all. Plus, knitting groups are a great way to socialize and make new friends. Imagine all the yarn-spinning, pattern-sharing goodness that awaits you!

Gardening is another great hobby for stress relief. It's a great way to get some fresh air and exercise, and there's something incredibly satisfying about watching your plants grow and flourish. Plus, you can use your homegrown fruits and veggies to impress your friends and family with your cooking skills. And if all else fails, you can always blame the bugs for your gardening failures.

Painting is another great option. It's a wonderful way to express yourself and can be very therapeutic. Plus, you never know, you might discover you have a talent for it! And if not, at least you have a colorful addition to your living room.

Starting a hobby is an easy way to reduce stress and meet new people with similar interests. So go out there and try something new, whether it's knitting, gardening, or painting. Who knows, you might just discover your new passion!

69. Reach out to old friends

Look no further than reaching out to old friends! Whether it's reconnecting with a childhood pal or catching up with an old colleague, reconnecting with people from your past can help build a sense of nostalgia and strengthen old connections.

Think about it, reminiscing about old memories and catching up on life can be an instant mood booster. It's like taking a trip down memory lane, but with the added bonus of having someone to share the experience with. Plus, who doesn't love a good "remember when" conversation?

And let's be real, we could all use some extra positivity in our lives. Especially during these times, where the world is a little more virtual than usual, having a friendly face to chat with can make all the difference.

But don't just take my word for it, try it out for yourself! Dust off that old address book and send a message to an old friend. You never know, they might be just as excited to hear from you as you are to hear from them. And if they're not? Well, at least you tried. And that's all that matters.

Or you could be like me and reach out to your old friends via social media. It's a great way to keep in touch with people from different countries, sometimes you can even find people you haven't seen for ages and it's a great way to find out what they're up to and how they've been.

So go ahead, take a break from the daily grind and reach out to an old friend. You never know, it just might be the stress-reliever you've been looking for.

70. Take a pet for a walk

Need a break from your daily routine? Well, I have the perfect solution for you: take a pet for a walk! Now, I know what you might be thinking, "But I don't have a pet." Well, that's okay! You can borrow a friend's pet, or even volunteer to walk a shelter dog. Trust me, the benefits of taking a pet for a walk are endless.

First of all, taking your furry friend for a stroll in the park or at the beach is a great way to get some fresh air and exercise. Not only will it improve your physical health, but it will also boost your mood and reduce your stress levels.

But that's not all, taking a pet for a walk can also be a great way to meet new people. Imagine this: you're out for a walk with your dog and you come across another dog-lover. They strike up a conversation with you and before you know it, you're making plans for a doggy playdate. See, taking a pet for a walk is like having your own personal ice-breaker.

And if you're feeling extra adventurous, you can even take your pet for a walk at the beach. Imagine the joy of watching your dog play in the waves, or the satisfaction of throwing a ball for them to fetch. Not only is it a great way to bond with your pet, but it's also a great way to bond with nature.

So, what are you waiting for? Grab a leash, call up a friend, or head to the nearest animal shelter and take a pet for a walk today. Not only will it improve your physical and mental health, but it will also give you the opportunity to make some new furry friends.?

Taking a pet for a walk can be a great way to reduce daily stress, meet new people, and bond over your shared love for animals. So, don't wait any longer, go out and enjoy a walk with your furry friend today! You might just find that it's the best stress-relieving activity you've ever tried.

71. Have a game night

Invite your loved ones over for a night filled with laughter and competition. Whether you prefer cards, board games, or video games, there's something for everyone.

For the traditionalists out there, break out the deck of cards and play a rousing game of poker or Go Fish. Feeling nostalgic? Dust off that Monopoly board and relive your childhood memories of fighting over Park Place and Boardwalk.

But don't think that game night is just for the older crowd. Grab your controllers and get ready to battle it out on the virtual battlefield in a heated game of Call of Duty or Mario Kart.

Not only is a game night a great way to bond with your loved ones, but it's also a stress-free way to spend an evening. Forget about the pressures of work and daily life and focus on the task at hand: dominating your opponents.

And if you're worried about running out of games to play, don't be. There's always something new to discover, whether it's a classic game with a twist or a brand new release. And if you're feeling adventurous, why not try making up your own game?

So gather your friends and family, break out the snacks and drinks, and get ready for a night of fun and laughter. Trust me, after a game night, you'll be feeling relaxed and refreshed, ready to take on the world.

72. Attend a festival or fair

Attending a festival or fair is a fantastic way to take a break from the daily grind and have some fun. Not only are they a great way to connect with people who share your interests, but they're also a great way to try new things and let loose.

Take a food festival, for example. Imagine strolling through rows of vendors, each one offering up a different delicious treat. You could try a new type of cuisine, sample some unique flavors, and even find a new favorite dish. And the best part? You don't have to worry about the dishes, because someone else is taking care of that for you!

Or maybe you're more of a music lover. A music festival is the perfect opportunity to see some of your favorite bands, discover new artists, and maybe even dance a little. And who doesn't love a good dance party? Whether you're grooving to the beat or just tapping your foot along, a music festival is a great way to let loose and have some fun.

And if you're more of a traditionalist, a county fair is the perfect choice for you. With everything from rides and games to farm animals and deep-fried goodies, a county fair has something for everyone. Plus, it's a great way to get a taste of rural life and enjoy some old-fashioned fun.

So why not take a break from your daily stress and attend a festival or fair? Whether you're a foodie, a music lover, or a traditionalist, there's something out there for everyone. And with so many options to choose from, you're sure to find something that strikes your fancy. Plus, it's a great way to add a little humor in your life, who knows what kind of funny situation you'll find yourself in.

So grab some friends, grab some sunscreen, and head out to your nearest festival or fair for a day of fun and laughter. Trust me, you won't regret it.

Building and maintaining a social support network takes time and effort, but it's worth it. Having a network of people you can turn to for support can help you navigate the ups and downs of life with a little more ease and a lot more laughter. So, don't be afraid to try out new things, put yourself out there and make connections with others. You never know who you might meet and how they might change your life for the better.

Self-Care

Self-care is a critical component of managing stress. It's all about taking the time to take care of yourself, both physically and emotionally. And the good news is, self-care doesn't have to be complicated or time-consuming. It can be as simple as taking a few minutes each day to do something that makes you feel good. Here are a few examples of how you can incorporate self-care into your daily routine.

First, let's talk about the basics. Getting enough sleep, eating a healthy diet, and staying active are all essential for maintaining good physical and emotional health. But let's face it, sometimes it's hard to make time for these things, especially when life gets hectic. That's why it's important to make self-care a priority.

For example, instead of hitting snooze and rushing out the door in the morning, try setting your alarm a little earlier and using that extra time to do something you enjoy, like reading a book or meditating. Instead of skipping breakfast or grabbing fast food on the go, try planning ahead and packing a healthy lunch or even better, preparing one the night before. And instead of sitting on the couch after a long day, try taking a walk or doing a quick workout.

But self-care isn't just about taking care of your physical health, it's also about taking care of your emotional well-being. One way to do this is by setting aside time each day to do something that makes you feel good. This could be anything from listening to music, to taking a bubble bath, to writing in a journal. The key is to find something that works for you and make it a regular part of your routine.

Another important aspect of self-care is learning to say no. We often put too much pressure on ourselves to do everything and please everyone. But the truth is, we can't do it all. So, it's important to learn to set boundaries and say no to things that don't align with our values or that we simply don't have the time or energy for.

Finally, don't forget to have fun! Life is short and we should enjoy it. So, make time for the things that bring you joy, whether it's playing a game, watching a movie, or going out with friends.

Self-care is about taking the time to take care of yourself, both physically and emotionally. It's about making self-care a priority, setting aside time each day to do something that makes you feel good, learning to say no, and having fun. Remember, you deserve it, and taking care of yourself is the first step towards managing stress in a positive and personal way.

73. Journaling

Writing down your thoughts and feelings can be a great way to process and release emotions. It's like having a therapist on call 24/7, except you don't have to pay by the hour or make small talk about the weather. Plus, it's a great way to reflect on your day and set intentions for the future.

For example, let's say you had a terrible day at work. Instead of bottling up those negative emotions, you can write them down in your journal. Get all of that pent-up anger and frustration out on the page. And the best part? You can tell your journal things you would never say to anyone else. It's like having a secret diary, but for adults.

Additionally, journaling is a great way to set intentions for the future. At the end of each day, you can reflect on what you accomplished and what you want to accomplish in the future. This can help you focus on your goals and make a plan to achieve them. It's like having a personal motivational coach, without the expensive fees.

But don't just take my word for it, give it a try yourself! And remember, don't take it too seriously. You don't have to write a Pulitzer Prize-winning novel every day. Just jot down a few sentences or doodles, whatever works for you. And who knows, you might even discover your inner Shakespeare or Picasso.

Journaling is a great way to process and release emotions, reflect on your day, and set intentions for the future. So grab a notebook and pen, and let the stress melt away!

74. Self-reflection

Self-reflection is like taking a mini vacation for your mind. It's a chance to step back from the chaos of everyday life and check in with yourself. It's like hitting the pause button on a hectic day and giving yourself some much-needed self-care. And the best part? It doesn't require a plane ticket or a fancy spa. All you need is a few minutes and a willingness to take a look at what's going on inside your head.

One way to practice self-reflection is to set aside some time each day to reflect on your thoughts and emotions. This can be done first thing in the morning, during lunch, or before bed. It's important to find a time that works best for you and make it a regular part of your routine.

During your self-reflection time, ask yourself questions like, "What am I feeling right now? Why am I feeling this way? What can I do to take care of myself in this moment?" These questions can help you identify what's causing you stress and what actions you can take to alleviate it.

For example, let's say you're feeling overwhelmed and stressed at work. During your self-reflection time, you might ask yourself, "Why am I feeling so stressed? Is it because I have too much on my plate? Is it because I'm not feeling supported by my team?" Once you've identified the root cause of your stress, you can take steps to address it. Maybe that means delegating some tasks, or having a conversation with your team about how they can support you better.

So next time you're feeling stressed and overwhelmed, remember to hit the pause button and take a few minutes to reflect on your thoughts and emotions. Trust me, your mind will thank you. And if all else fails, just remember that self-reflection is like a mini vacation for your mind - and who doesn't love a good vacation?

75. Meditation

Let's face it, life can be pretty hectic. Between work, family, and trying to fit in a social life, it can feel like there's never a moment to just sit back and relax. But what if I told you that by simply sitting still and focusing on your breath, you could reduce stress, quiet your mind, and improve your overall well-being? Sounds too good to be true, right? Well, my friend, that's the power of meditation.

Now, I know what you might be thinking. "But I can't meditate! I can't sit still for more than 5 seconds without my mind racing." Trust me, I get it. I used to be the same way. But the beauty of meditation is that it's not about clearing your mind completely (that's basically impossible), it's about acknowledging your thoughts and letting them pass by without getting caught up in them. It's like watching a river flow by, you can see the water, but you don't get pulled in.

So, how do you get started with meditation? Well, first things first, you need to find a comfortable spot. This can be anywhere, from a quiet room in your house to a park bench. Once you're comfortable, all you need to do is focus on your breath. That's it. Just breathe in, breathe out. You can also count your breaths if that helps to keep your mind from wandering.

Now, I know this might sound a little boring, but hear me out. When you're focusing on your breath, you're bringing your attention to the present moment. And when you're in the present moment, you're not worrying about the past or the future. This can help to reduce stress and anxiety because you're not dwelling on things you can't change or worrying about things that haven't happened yet.

And if you're still not convinced, consider the benefits. Studies have shown that meditation can lower blood pressure, improve sleep, and even boost your immune system. Not to mention, it's a great way to relax and find some inner peace.

So, the next time you're feeling stressed out, take a few minutes to sit still and focus on your breath. Who knows, you might just find that a little bit of meditation can go a long way in reducing stress and improving your overall well-being. And remember, if your mind starts to wander, just think of it as a river flowing by, and let it pass on by.

76. Reading

That's right, folks, the simple act of picking up a good book and diving into its pages can be a great way to relax and unwind after a long day.

Now, I know what you might be thinking. " I don't have time to read!" Well, my dear friend, you don't need to dedicate hours upon hours to reading in order to reap the benefits. Just a few minutes each day can make a big difference. Think of it like taking a mini vacation without ever leaving your couch.

Now, you might be wondering what kind of book you should be reading in order to de-stress. The answer is simple: whatever you enjoy! Whether it's a page-turning thriller, a heartwarming romance, or a non-fiction book that teaches you something new, the important thing is that it's something you find interesting.

For example, if you're someone who loves a good mystery, why not pick up Agatha Christie's "Murder on the Orient Express"? The twists and turns of the story will keep you on the edge of your seat, and before you know it, you'll have forgotten all about the stresses of your day.

Or, if you're someone who enjoys learning new things, try reading "The Art of War" by Sun Tzu. Not only will you learn about strategy and tactics, but you'll also gain a new perspective on the world around you.

And for those who love to laugh, try reading "Where'd You Go, Bernadette" by Maria Semple. It is a hilarious story that will make you forget all your worries, with a side of witty sarcasm.

So, there you have it, folks. Next time you're feeling stressed, don't reach for that bottle of wine or that bag of chips. Reach for a book instead. Trust me, your mind (and waistline) will thank you.

77. Music

Let me tell you something: music is the ultimate stress-buster. It's like a magic wand that can instantly transport you to a happy place, far away from the worries of daily life. Whether you're feeling down in the dumps or just need a pick-me-up, a good song can work wonders.

First things first, if you want to reduce stress, you need to have a go-to list of songs that make you feel good. Think of it as your personal anti-anxiety playlist. Mine, for example, includes classics like "I Will Survive" by Gloria Gaynor and "Don't Stop Believin'" by Journey. These songs never fail to put a smile on my face and get me dancing like nobody's watching (even though they totally are).

Another great idea is to create a playlist specifically for self-care. This can include soothing songs like "Weightless" by Marconi Union, or uplifting tracks like "Brave" by Sara Bareilles. You can even add in some guided meditations or nature sounds for added relaxation.

But don't stop there! Experiment with different genres and discover new music that makes you feel good. For me, that means jamming out to some old-school hip-hop or indie rock. And let's not forget about the power of a good sing-along. Whether you're belting out the lyrics in the shower or having a karaoke night with friends, singing is a great way to release stress and have fun.

Music is a powerful tool for self-care and stress-relief. So next time you're feeling overwhelmed, put on your favorite tune and let the good vibes flow. And remember, if life gives you lemons, make a playlist of upbeat songs and dance it out.

78. Cooking

Cooking is a fantastic way to relax and unwind after a long day. Not only do you get to create something delicious and satisfying, but you also get to enjoy the fruits of your labor. Plus, if you're looking to reduce daily stress, cooking can be a great way to do that.

One way to reduce stress through cooking is to prepare a healthy meal. Instead of ordering takeout or grabbing something from a drive-thru, spend some time in the kitchen whipping up a delicious and nutritious meal. For example, you could make a quinoa salad with black beans and roasted vegetables. Not only is it packed with protein and healthy fats, but it's also delicious and satisfying.

Another way to reduce stress through cooking is to bake your favorite treat. Baking is a great way to relax and unwind, and the smell of freshly baked cookies or brownies can be incredibly soothing. Plus, it's hard to be stressed when you're indulging in a warm, gooey chocolate chip cookie straight out of the oven.

But sometimes you just want to indulge in something sweet, and that's totally okay. So if you want to bake a cake, cookies or any other sweet treat go for it. Just remember to enjoy every bite and savor the flavor.

Cooking can be a great way to reduce daily stress, whether you're preparing a healthy meal or baking your favorite treat. So, put on your apron, turn on some music, and let the stress melt away in the kitchen.

79. Watching a funny movie or TV show

Laughter is truly the best medicine. And what better way to get your daily dose than by watching a funny movie or TV show? Not only is it a great way to take a break and relax, but it also has some amazing benefits for your mental and physical well-being.

Think about it, when you're laughing, your body is releasing endorphins, which are the "feel-good" chemicals in your brain. They help reduce pain, improve your mood and can even boost your immune system. So, instead of popping a pill, pop in a comedy DVD or turn on your favorite sitcom.

But, with so many options out there, it can be hard to know where to start. Don't worry, I've got you covered. If you're looking for something classic and timeless, I highly recommend "I Love Lucy." Lucille Ball's comedic timing is impeccable and it's hard not to laugh at her antics. If you're more of a fan of slapstick humor, "The Three Stooges" is sure to have you in stitches.

If you're in the mood for something a little more contemporary, I suggest checking out "Parks and Recreation." The show is filled with clever jokes and the characters are all lovable in their own unique way. And let's not forget about "Brooklyn Nine-Nine," a show that will have you laughing and crying at the same time.

And don't forget, laughter is contagious, so grab a friend or family member and make it a group activity. Not only will you be reducing your daily stress, but you'll also be bonding with your loved ones.

So, don't wait any longer. Put down that stress ball and pick up the remote. Trust me, your soul (and your abs) will thank you.

80. Relaxing bath

The never-ending to-do list, the constant barrage of notifications, and the constant chatter in your head all combine to make you want to pull your hair out. Well, I have the solution for you: a relaxing bath.

First things first, let's set the scene. Light some candles, dim the lights, and put on some soft music. Not sure what music to choose? How about some classical music to soothe your soul or some nature sounds to transport you to a peaceful forest. Now, let's talk about bath time essentials. A nice bubble bath is always a good idea, but if you're feeling extra fancy, why not add some Epsom salts or essential oils to take your bath to the next level.

Now, it's time to sink into the warm water and let all your troubles melt away. Close your eyes and let your mind wander. Imagine yourself on a tropical island, lounging on a hammock with a cold drink in your hand. Or maybe you're floating in the ocean, watching the sunset and feeling the gentle waves rock you to sleep.

It's important to remember that this is your time, so don't let anyone or anything interrupt you. Turn off your phone, lock the door and let yourself fully relax. Trust me, when you get out of the bath, you'll feel like a brand new person.

So, next time you're feeling overwhelmed, don't hesitate to run yourself a relaxing bath. It's a great way to unwind and de-stress, and honestly, who doesn't love a good soak in the tub? Don't forget to bring a good book or magazine, or even a glass of wine to complete the ultimate relaxation experience. Just make sure you don't fall asleep and drown, that would be a real bummer.

81. Massage

How many times have you come home from a long day at work, your shoulders knotted up and your mind racing, and thought to yourself, "Man, I could really use a massage right now"? I know I have. And let me tell you, there's nothing quite like the feeling of someone working out all the tension and stress from your body. It's like they're magically erasing all the bad parts of your day and replacing them with pure, unadulterated relaxation.

Now, I know what you might be thinking. "But wait, massages are expensive! I can't afford to treat myself to one every time I'm feeling stressed out." And sure, regular massages can be pricey. But that doesn't mean you can't enjoy the benefits of a good massage without breaking the bank.

First of all, there's the good old-fashioned self-massage. You don't need to be a trained masseuse to give yourself a little rubdown. Just grab some lotion or oil and start working out the kinks in your muscles. You'd be surprised how much tension you can release just by using your own hands.

Another option is to look into community massage events or pop-up massage stations. These events often offer massages at a reduced rate, and they're a great way to get a quick pick-me up without having to commit to a full-length session.

And let's not forget the power of a good, old-fashioned hug. Sometimes, all you need is a little human touch to make you feel better. So go hug someone you love, or even better, ask them to give you a massage! Just make sure you return the favor.

Don't let the cost of a massage keep you from treating yourself to one. There are plenty of ways to get the benefits of a massage without breaking the bank. So go ahead, give yourself a little rubdown and let all that stress and tension melt away.

82. Aromatherapy

Aromatherapy is a wonderful way to create a relaxing atmosphere and reduce daily stress. Essential oils have been used for centuries to promote relaxation, reduce anxiety, and improve overall well-being. Whether you're looking to unwind after a long day at work or create a peaceful ambiance in your home, essential oils can help.

One of the best ways to use essential oils for aromatherapy is through a diffuser. A diffuser disperses the oils into the air, allowing you to breathe in the benefits. Simply add a few drops of your favorite essential oil to the diffuser, turn it on, and sit back and relax.

Some of my favorite essential oils for relaxation include lavender, chamomile, and vanilla. Lavender is known for its calming properties, and is often used to help with insomnia and anxiety. Chamomile is also a great option for relaxation, and is often used to help with insomnia and anxiety. Vanilla is a comforting and soothing scent that can help to reduce stress and promote feelings of calm.

Another great way to use essential oils for aromatherapy is by adding them to your bath. Simply add a few drops of your favorite essential oil to your bathwater, and let the oils infuse into the water. As you soak, you'll be able to breathe in the benefits of the oils, and your skin will absorb them as well. This is a perfect way to relax after a long day at work, or to unwind before bed.

And let's not forget the power of a good old fashioned massage. Mix a few drops of your favorite essential oil with a carrier oil (such as coconut or almond oil) and give yourself or a loved one a relaxing massage. Not only will the oils help to relax your muscles and reduce stress, but the massage itself will also help to promote relaxation.

In conclusion, Aromatherapy is not only a way to make your home smell like a fancy spa, but it's also a natural and effective way to reduce daily stress and promote relaxation. So, go ahead, break out the diffuser, light some candles, and let the essential oils work their magic. And remember, if all else fails, just add some lavender oil to your bath, and imagine yourself in a field of lavender in the south of France.

83. Plan a day off or a weekend getaway

Are you feeling burnt out from the daily grind? It's time to take a break and plan a day off or a weekend getaway. Trust me, a little R&R is just what the doctor ordered to reduce stress and rejuvenate your mind, body, and soul.

For starters, imagine waking up without an alarm clock blaring in your ear. No rush to get ready for work, no traffic to deal with, just the sound of birds chirping and the smell of fresh coffee. That alone is enough to make anyone feel more relaxed.

Now, let's talk about the actual day off or weekend getaway. The options are endless! You could take a hike in the mountains, lay on the beach, or even just stay in bed all day and catch up on your favorite TV shows. The point is, do whatever makes YOU happy.

But if you need some inspiration, let me give you some ideas:

- Take a hot air balloon ride and watch the sunrise
- Visit a nearby winery and taste some delicious wines
- Go to a spa and treat yourself to a massage or facial
- Rent a cabin in the woods and unplug from technology for a while
- Take a cooking class and learn how to make a new dish
- Explore a nearby city you've never been to before

Whatever you choose to do, make sure you disconnect from the daily routine and enjoy your time off. And remember, a change of scenery can do wonders for the mind and body.

Don't wait to plan that day off or weekend getaway. It's the perfect way to relax, de-stress, and come back to your daily life feeling refreshed and ready to tackle any challenges that come your way. So, pack your bags and let's hit the road, baby!

These self-care practices can be tailored to your personal needs and preferences. Remember, self-care is not a luxury, it's a necessity.

Mindset

Stress and negative thinking often go hand in hand. When we're feeling stressed, it can be easy to fall into the trap of negative thoughts and self-doubt. But the good news is, we have the power to change our thoughts and, in turn, reduce our stress levels. Here's a look at the link between stress and negative thinking, and some examples of how to shift your thinking in a more positive direction.

First, let's talk about the link between stress and negative thinking. When we're stressed, our body releases the hormone cortisol, which can make us feel anxious and on edge. And when we're feeling anxious, it can be easy to fall into the trap of negative thoughts, such as "I can't do this," "I'm not good enough," or "This is never going to work out." These negative thoughts can fuel our stress and make it even harder to cope.

So, how can we shift our thinking in a more positive direction? One way is through mindfulness. Mindfulness is the practice of being present in the moment and observing our thoughts without judgment. By becoming aware of our thoughts, we can begin to identify negative patterns and make a conscious effort to shift them.

Another way to shift our thinking is through reframing. Reframing is the process of looking at a situation in a different way. For example, instead of thinking, "This is never going to work out," we can reframe our thoughts and say, "This may be difficult, but I'll find a way to make it work."

We can also use affirmations to shift our thinking. Affirmations are positive statements that we repeat to ourselves. For example, instead of thinking "I'm not good enough," we can repeat the affirmation, "I am capable and worthy."

Finally, it's important to challenge negative thoughts when they arise. Ask yourself, "Is this thought based on fact or is it just a negative assumption?" "Can I find evidence to support this thought or is it just a negative interpretation?" "How would I think or feel about this situation if I had a more positive mindset?"

Stress and negative thinking often go hand in hand, but by becoming aware of our thoughts, reframing them, using affirmations and challenging them, we can reduce our stress levels and improve our overall well being. Remember, it's not about always having positive thoughts, but about not getting stuck in negative thoughts, and it's also important to not take yourself too seriously and add a touch of humor in the process.

84. Gratitude

Gratitude is like a superpower that can help you shift your focus to the positive things in your life and reduce daily stress. One simple yet powerful way to harness the power of gratitude is by starting a gratitude journal. Here's how it works: each day, take a few minutes to write down three things you're grateful for. It can be something as small as a delicious cup of coffee in the morning or as big as a loving family.

Now, I know what you might be thinking, " I already have so much on my plate, how am I supposed to find time to write in a journal every day?" Well, my friend, that's the beauty of it! This gratitude journal doesn't require much time or effort. You can do it while you're waiting in line at the grocery store, or before you go to bed at night. It's a small and easy step that can make a big difference in your life.

But don't just take my word for it, try it out for yourself! You'll be surprised how quickly you'll start noticing the good things in your life. And who knows, maybe you'll even find yourself saying "Thank you" for introducing you to this life-changing habit.

Just a warning though, once you start your gratitude journal, you might find yourself becoming a gratitude-journal-addict, like me. I mean, who doesn't like feeling good and positive?. It's like a drug but legal, cheaper and healthier.

85. Reframing

Reframing is the secret weapon in the battle against daily stress. Instead of dwelling on the negative, it's all about finding that silver lining, or the positive aspect in a difficult situation.

For example, let's say you're stuck in traffic on the way to work. You could sit there, cursing the cars in front of you, and the construction that's causing the delay. Or, you could reframe the situation and think, "Wow, I have a car that's working, and I'm on my way to a job that pays me money. I'm one lucky person!"

Or, let's say you've got a big presentation at work and you're feeling the pressure. Instead of freaking out and thinking "I'm going to mess this up and they're going to hate me", reframe the situation and think "This is an opportunity for me to show off my skills and impress my colleagues. I've got this!"

Reframing can also be helpful in personal relationships. Let's say your partner is being particularly grumpy and it's getting on your nerves. Instead of getting angry and thinking "they're being such a jerk", reframe the situation and think "they must be having a tough day, I'll give them some space and offer my support later."

The point is, when we reframe a situation, we're not ignoring the problem or pretending it doesn't exist. We're just choosing to focus on the positive aspects, rather than dwelling on the negative. And trust me, when you start looking for the good in every situation, you'll be amazed at how much less stressed you feel.

And hey, if all else fails and you can't find anything positive, just remember - at least you're not stuck in a traffic jam on the way to a job you hate, with a partner who's always grumpy. So, chin up buttercup!

86. Positive affirmations

These little mantras can do wonders for reducing daily stress and making you feel like you can conquer the world. Now, I know some of you may be thinking, "I already know that I am worthy and capable. Why do I need to repeat it to myself?" Well, my dear friends, it's not just about knowing it, it's about internalizing it and truly believing it.

Think of it like this: if you're trying to build muscle, you don't just look at pictures of buff dudes and think "Wow, I want to look like that." No, you hit the gym, you lift weights, you eat protein-rich foods, and you repeat the process over and over again. It's the same with positive affirmations. By repeating them to yourself daily, you're training your brain to believe them and make them a part of your subconscious.

But what kind of affirmations should you be saying? Well, they can be as simple as "I am worthy" or "I am capable." Or, if you're feeling a little more adventurous, you can try some like "I am surrounded by love and support," "I choose to focus on the positive," or "I am confident in my abilities." The possibilities are endless!

Now, I know some of you may be thinking, "This sounds a little too good to be true. How can a few words really change my life?" Well, my friends, it's all about perspective. If you're constantly telling yourself negative things, like "I'll never be good enough," or "I can't handle this," then you're setting yourself up for failure. But if you're telling yourself positive things, like "I am strong," or "I can handle this," then you're setting yourself up for success.

So, my dear friends, I urge you to give positive affirmations a try. You may be surprised at how much of a difference a few simple words can make in your life. And hey, if all else fails, you can always just repeat "I am worthy of a good cup of coffee" and see if that helps.

87. Surround yourself with positive people

It's no secret that the people we surround ourselves with can have a huge impact on our overall well-being. That's why, if you're looking to reduce daily stress, it's essential to surround yourself with positive people. But what does that even mean?

Well, for starters, it means spending time with people who uplift and inspire you. These are the folks who make you feel good about yourself and your abilities. They're the ones who believe in you, even when you don't believe in yourself. They're the ones who give you a much-needed pep talk when you're feeling down. And they're the ones who make you laugh until your sides hurt.

Now, I know what you might be thinking: "But what if I don't have any positive people in my life?" Trust me, they're out there. They might be hiding in plain sight, like that colleague who always has a kind word to say, or that neighbor who's always willing to lend a hand. Or they might be waiting to be discovered, like that new friend you meet at a meetup or that stranger who strikes up a conversation on the bus.

Once you've found your positive posse, make sure to spend as much time with them as possible. Hang out, grab a coffee, go for a walk, or simply chat on the phone. Trust me, their positive energy is contagious and you'll soon find yourself feeling more uplifted and inspired than ever before.

Now, I know what you might be thinking: "But what if I don't have time to spend with these positive people?" My friend, you make time. Whether it's getting up an hour earlier, staying up an hour later, or taking a lunch break when you're not really hungry, you'll find a way.

And if you're still feeling stressed? It's time to call in the big guns. I'm talking about those ultimate stress-busters: the ones who can make you forget all your troubles with just one laugh. Yes, I'm talking about your comedic squad. These are the people who can make you laugh until you cry and forget all your worries.

So don't be afraid to let them in your life, they're the ones that will make you forget why you were stressed in the first place.

If you want to reduce daily stress, surround yourself with positive people. Spend time with people who uplift and inspire you, and make sure to have some comedic squad around you too. Positive energy is contagious, and with the right people in your life, you'll be well on your way to a stress-free existence.

88. Practice self-compassion

Self-compassion is the key to reducing daily stress and living a happier life. It's the act of being kind and understanding towards yourself, especially during difficult times. We all make mistakes and have setbacks, it's part of being human. But, it's important to remember that these setbacks are not a reflection of our worth as a person.

Think about it this way, would you say the same things to your best friend that you say to yourself in your head? Probably not. So, why not treat yourself with the same kindness and understanding that you would show to your loved ones?

For example, let's say you're having a bad day at work and you spilled coffee on your shirt. Instead of berating yourself and calling yourself clumsy, try saying something like "Hey, it happens to the best of us. I'll just change my shirt and power through the day."

Or, let's say you didn't meet your workout goals for the week. Instead of calling yourself lazy, try saying something like "I didn't meet my goals this week, but I'm proud of the progress I've made so far and I'll keep working towards them."

Another example, let's say you didn't finish a project in time, instead of calling yourself a failure, try saying something like "I did my best, I'll learn from my mistakes and do better next time."

By practicing self-compassion, you're allowing yourself to acknowledge your mistakes and setbacks without letting them define you. It's like giving yourself a virtual pat on the back, reminding yourself that you're human and you're doing the best you can. And remember, if you're not kind to yourself, who will be?

So next time, when something goes wrong, don't beat yourself up, just remind yourself that you're human and it's okay to make mistakes. And remember, the only way to avoid mistakes is to do nothing, and where's the fun in that?

89. Find humor in the situation

Laughter is the best medicine, and there's nothing like a good dose of humor to shift your mindset and reduce stress. We've all heard the saying, "find the silver lining," but what if we took that a step further and actively sought out humor in even the most trying of situations? Trust me, it's not as difficult as it sounds.

For example, let's say you're stuck in traffic. Instead of getting frustrated and letting your stress levels rise, try to find something humorous about the situation. Maybe the driver in the car next to you has a ridiculous bumper sticker or there's a llama in the back of a pickup truck. These small, unexpected moments of levity can go a long way in taking the edge off a frustrating situation.

Another example, imagine you're in a meeting at work and it's not going well. Rather than getting bogged down in the negativity, try to find the humor in it. Maybe the person leading the meeting is using a terrible PowerPoint template or a colleague keeps using buzzwords that make no sense. These little moments of absurdity can be a great source of stress relief.

Even something as simple as finding humor in your own mistakes can be incredibly beneficial. We've all been there - spilling coffee on ourselves, tripping over our own feet, etc. Instead of getting embarrassed and stressed out, try to see the humor in the situation. You'll feel much better, and the people around you will appreciate your ability to laugh at yourself.

Finding humor in the situation is key to shifting your mindset and reducing stress. Remember, laughter truly is the best medicine, so don't be afraid to seek it out, even in the most trying of situations. Trust me, you'll be glad you did.

90. Practice random acts of kindness

We all have those days where everything seems to be going wrong and we can't shake off the stress. But what if I told you that there's a simple solution to boost your mood and reduce stress? It's called "Practicing Random Acts of Kindness"!

Here's how it works: You do something nice for someone else. It can be as small as holding the door open for someone or as big as paying for a stranger's coffee. The point is, by doing something nice for someone else, you're not only making their day a little bit brighter, but you're also giving yourself a little mood boost.

Need some inspiration? Here are a few examples:

Leave a note of encouragement on a co-worker's desk when they're having a tough day.
Pay for the person's meal behind you in the drive-thru line.
Leave some extra change in the vending machine for the next person.
Compliment a stranger on something they're wearing.
Offer to walk a neighbor's dog if they're feeling under the weather.
The possibilities are endless! And the best part is, you don't have to spend a lot of money or make a big fuss. Sometimes, the smallest acts of kindness can make the biggest impact.

So the next time you're feeling stressed or down, try practicing a random act of kindness. I guarantee it will not only make someone else's day, but it will also give you a little boost and help you feel good about yourself. Plus, who doesn't love a good excuse to spread some positivity in the world? So go forth, my friends, and make the world a kinder place, one random act at a time!

91. Practice forgiveness

Forgiveness is like a magical stress-relieving potion that you can brew up in your own mind. It's the ultimate way to let go of grudges and resentment, and to stop those negative feelings from hurting you. But, like any potion, it takes practice to master.

First, let's talk about the benefits of forgiveness. Holding onto grudges and resentment is like carrying a heavy bag of bricks around with you all day. It's exhausting! But when you forgive, it's like someone came along and took away all those bricks, leaving you feeling light as a feather.

But, here's the thing, forgiveness doesn't mean you have to forget what happened or that you have to be friends with the person who wronged you. It just means that you're choosing to let go of the negative feelings and move on with your life. And let me tell you, it feels amazing.

Now, for the practice part. Think of forgiveness like a muscle, the more you use it, the stronger it becomes. Start small, maybe there's a co-worker who always borrows your stapler and never brings it back. Instead of getting angry every time, forgive them and remind yourself that it's just a stapler. Or maybe there's a family member who always says hurtful things. Instead of holding onto the resentment, forgive them and focus on the positive aspects of your relationship.

As you get better at forgiveness, you can work your way up to bigger things. But remember, forgiveness is not about the other person, it's about you and your own peace of mind.

92. Make time for yourself

Life can be hectic, can't it? Between work, family, and social obligations, it can be hard to find a moment to yourself. But did you know that taking a little bit of time each day to do something you enjoy can help reduce stress and improve your overall well-being? It's true!

Here's an example: imagine you've had a long day at the office. You're feeling frazzled and just want to collapse on the couch. But instead of zoning out in front of the TV, you set aside 30 minutes to do something you love. Maybe it's reading a book, taking a yoga class, or even just going for a walk around the block.

By taking that time to focus on yourself and do something you enjoy, you're giving your mind and body a chance to relax and recharge. And when you're feeling more relaxed and refreshed, you're better equipped to handle the challenges of the day.

Another example is, imagine you're a busy stay-at-home mom and you're constantly juggling the needs of your kids, your partner, and your home. It can be easy to forget to take care of yourself. But setting aside even just 15 minutes a day to do something you enjoy can make a big difference. Maybe it's taking a relaxing bath, listening to music or even just sitting down and having a cup of tea.

Whatever it is, taking that time to focus on yourself can help you feel more balanced and less stressed. And when you're less stressed, you're better able to take care of those around you. So go ahead and make time for yourself, you deserve it!

93. Live in the present

Are you tired of constantly dwelling on the past and worrying about the future? Do you find yourself feeling stressed and overwhelmed on a daily basis? Well, my friend, it's time to take a step back and start living in the present moment.

The past is gone and the future is yet to come, so why waste your precious time and energy on things you can't change or control? Instead, focus on the present and make the most of it.

One way to do this is by practicing mindfulness. This can be as simple as taking a few deep breaths, focusing on your surroundings, and being present in the moment. You can also try activities like yoga, meditation, or journaling to help you stay in the present.

Another way to live in the present is to find joy in the little things. Instead of always looking for the next big thing, take a moment to appreciate the beauty of a sunset, the taste of a delicious meal, or the laughter of a friend.

And when regrets from the past or worries about the future do creep in, try to reframe them with a bit of humor. For example, instead of beating yourself up over a mistake you made in the past, remind yourself that everyone makes mistakes and that it's a part of being human. And when worrying about the future, remind yourself that worrying about things that haven't happened yet is like paying interest on a debt you may never owe.

So, my friend, don't get bogged down by regrets of the past or worries about the future. Live in the present moment and enjoy it. Trust me, it's a lot more fun than dwelling on the past or worrying about the future.

94. Learn something new

Are you feeling stressed out and in need of a mental break? Look no further than learning something new! Whether it's taking a class, reading a book, or trying a new hobby, the benefits of learning are endless. Not only does it keep the mind active and sharp, but it can also shift your focus to the positive and help reduce daily stress.

For example, if you're feeling overwhelmed at work, why not take a cooking class to learn some new recipes? Not only will you impress your coworkers with your newfound culinary skills, but you'll also have something delicious to look forward to at the end of a long day.

Or maybe you're feeling a bit down and in need of some inspiration. Pick up a book on a topic that interests you, whether it's science, history, or even fiction. Reading can transport you to a different time and place, and provide a welcome escape from the daily grind.

If you're looking for a more hands-on approach, why not try a new hobby? Take up painting, knitting, or even rock climbing. Not only will you learn something new, but you'll also get a sense of accomplishment from creating something beautiful or conquering a new challenge.

So if you're feeling stressed, don't let it get you down. Take a class, read a book, or try a new hobby. You never know, you might just discover a new passion or skill. And who knows, you might even be able to turn that hobby into a side hustle and make some extra cash while you're at it!

95. Practice being more optimistic

Well, it's time to turn that frown upside down and start practicing being more optimistic! Instead of focusing on the negative, try to see the good in situations.

Let's take a common scenario: you're stuck in traffic and running late for an appointment. Instead of getting angry and frustrated, try to see the silver lining. Maybe you needed a break from your busy schedule, or you'll get to hear your favorite song on the radio.

Another example: a coworker didn't turn in a report on time, causing you to stay late at the office. Instead of getting mad at them, try to see it as an opportunity to bond with your coworkers over some pizza and a good laugh.

Or let's say you got a bad grade on a test. Instead of dwelling on it and feeling down, try to see it as a learning opportunity and a chance to do better next time.

Now, I know it's not always easy to think positive, especially when things are tough. But trust me, it's worth it. When you're able to see the good in situations, it can reduce your stress levels and make you a happier person overall. Plus, people will be attracted to your positive energy, and who doesn't want that? So next time you're feeling down, try to find the good in the situation. And if all else fails, just remember: "Every cloud has a silver lining" and if not, there is always a rainbow after the rain.

96. Surround yourself with positivity

Life can be tough, and sometimes the stress of everyday living can feel overwhelming. One way to combat this stress is by surrounding yourself with positivity. This doesn't mean you have to go out and buy a "Happiness Is a Choice" poster, but keeping positive quotes, images, or anything that makes you feel good around you can help shift your focus to the positive and remind you of what's important.

For example, if you're someone who likes to keep a daily planner, why not write a positive quote on the top of each page? It'll be the first thing you see when you open your planner and can help set the tone for the day. Or maybe you're someone who likes to have a screensaver on your phone. Instead of a picture of your cat, why not use an image that inspires you or makes you smile?

Another way to surround yourself with positivity is by keeping a gratitude journal. Each day, write down three things you're grateful for. It doesn't have to be big things, it can be something as simple as "I'm grateful for my morning coffee" or "I'm grateful for the sunshine today." By focusing on the positive, you'll start to notice more and more things to be grateful for.

And, if you're feeling really adventurous, why not try a vision board? A vision board is a collage of images, quotes, and other items that represent the life you want to create. It's like a Pinterest board come to life. You can put it in your office, your bedroom, or anywhere you'll see it often. It's a constant reminder of what you're working towards and can help keep you motivated.

So, if you're feeling stressed and need a little pick-me-up, try surrounding yourself with positivity. It's like a personal cheer squad, always there to remind you that you've got this. And remember, as the famous quote goes, "Positive vibes only please."

Remember, developing a positive mindset takes time and effort, but with practice, you can learn to shift your focus to the positive, reduce stress and improve overall well-being. It's also important to not take yourself too seriously and to add a touch of humor in the process. These are examples of things you can do to improve your mindset, and remember you can always find your own way to develop your own positive mindset.

Sleep

When it comes to stress and poor sleep, it can feel like a never-ending cycle of tossing and turning. You're stressed out, so you can't fall asleep. And then you can't sleep, so you're even more stressed out. But the truth is, stress and poor sleep are closely linked and it's important to address both in order to improve overall well-being.

I know from personal experience how hard it can be to fall asleep when my mind is racing with thoughts about work, family, and the never-ending to-do list. And I'm sure many of you can relate. But just because it's common, doesn't mean it's healthy. Chronic stress and poor sleep can lead to all sorts of problems, from a weakened immune system to an increased risk of chronic diseases.

So, what can we do about it? Well, for starters, we can try to relax. Easier said than done, I know. But there are a few things that have worked for me and could work for you too.

97. Stick to a regular sleep schedule

Are you tired of feeling like a zombie during the day? Do you find yourself constantly reaching for that extra cup of coffee just to make it through the day? Well, have no fear because I have the solution for you. The key to reducing daily stress and feeling refreshed is to stick to a regular sleep schedule.

Now, I know what you may be thinking. "I deserve to sleep in on the weekends after a long week of work." And I totally agree, you do deserve it. But, hear me out. Consistency is key when it comes to setting your body's internal clock. Going to bed and waking up at the same time every day, even on weekends, will help regulate your body's sleep-wake cycle and make it easier for you to fall asleep and wake up.

Think about it like this, if you're used to going to bed at 11 PM on weekdays and then sleep until noon on weekends, your body doesn't know when it's supposed to be asleep or awake. But, if you stick to a consistent schedule of say, going to bed at 10 PM and waking up at 6 AM every day, your body will quickly adjust to the schedule and make it easier for you to fall asleep and wake up.

And trust me, the benefits of sticking to a regular sleep schedule are worth it. You'll have more energy during the day, be more productive, and even have a better mood. And let's not forget, you'll also be able to say goodbye to those dark circles under your eyes.

So, go ahead and set that alarm for the same time every day, even on weekends. And don't worry, if you're still feeling groggy in the morning, just remember, at least you'll look well-rested. Happy Zzz-ing!

98. Develop a bedtime ritual

Let me introduce you to the magical world of bedtime rituals.

Now, I know what you might be thinking. "I already brush my teeth and wash my face before bed. Is that not enough of a ritual?" Unfortunately, my dear friends, that is not quite enough to signal to your body that it's time to wind down.

Let me give you an example of what a bedtime ritual might look like. Imagine, you come home from a long day of work and instead of immediately collapsing on the couch and scrolling through your phone, you take a warm bath with some lavender essential oils. As you soak, you listen to some calming music, maybe even some whale songs if that's your thing. After your bath, you grab a book and spend some time reading before you finally crawl into bed.

Or maybe, your ritual is more of a physical one. You spend some time stretching and doing some yoga before bed, or even writing in a journal to process your thoughts from the day.

The point is, having a bedtime ritual is a way to signal to your body that it's time to wind down. It's a way to tell your brain "Hey, it's time to stop thinking about work and all the things we have to do tomorrow, it's time to relax and get some rest."

And trust me, when you have a consistent bedtime ritual, you'll be sleeping like a baby in no time. And who doesn't want to sleep like a baby? Well, maybe not the actual baby, but you get the point.

So go forth, my friends, and develop your own bedtime ritual. Whether it's reading, yoga, or even just a cup of tea, make it something that you look forward to every night. And hey, if all else fails, you can always try counting sheep. But let's be real, that never works.

99. Create a sleep-friendly environment

Do you wake up feeling groggy and irritable? Well, have no fear, because I'm here to give you some tips on how to create the ultimate sleep-friendly environment.

First things first, let's talk temperature. Your bedroom should be cool, not too warm and not too cold. I mean, have you ever tried to sleep when it feels like you're in a sauna? It's not pleasant, trust me. So, invest in a good air conditioner or a fan to keep that room at a comfortable temperature.

Next, let's talk about light. Darkness is key when it comes to sleep. I mean, you're not trying to catch a tan while you're catching some z's, are you? So, invest in some black-out curtains or a sleep mask if your room is too bright. And, while we're on the topic of light, make sure to turn off all electronic devices at least an hour before bedtime. You know, that blue light they emit messes with your sleep.
Last, but not least, let's talk about noise. A quiet environment is essential for a good night's sleep. I mean, have you ever tried to sleep with a drill going on outside your window? Not fun. So, invest in some earplugs or a white noise machine if your neighborhood is too noisy.

And, let's not forget about bedding. Make sure you have a comfortable mattress, pillows, and sheets. I mean, you're going to be spending a third of your life in bed, so you might as well make it a pleasant experience.

So, there you have it folks, the ultimate guide to creating a sleep-friendly environment. Now, go forth and sleep like a baby!

100. Avoid stimulating activities before bed

Do you find yourself staring at the ceiling, counting sheep, or scrolling through your phone for hours on end? Well, I've got some bad news for you, my friend. The problem might not be your mattress or your pillow, but rather the things you're doing before bedtime.

You see, when it comes to sleep, timing is everything. And if you're engaging in stimulating activities before bed, you're setting yourself up for a long night of frustration. So, if you want to reduce your daily stress and get a better night's sleep, you need to avoid the following three things: screens, caffeine, and heavy meals close to bedtime.

Let's start with screens. Whether it's your phone, your tablet, your laptop, or your TV, screens emit a blue light that can mess with your body's natural sleep-wake cycle. This blue light tricks your brain into thinking it's daytime, making it harder for you to fall asleep and stay asleep. So, if you want to avoid this, you should put away all screens at least an hour before bed.

Next up, caffeine. I know, I know. You're thinking, "How am I supposed to survive the day without my morning cup of joe?" Well, the thing is, caffeine can stay in your system for up to eight hours, so even if you're drinking your coffee in the morning, it can still affect your sleep at night. So, if you want to avoid this, you should cut off caffeine consumption at least six hours before bed.

Finally, heavy meals close to bedtime. Eating a big meal before bed can cause indigestion and acid reflux, which can make it hard for you to sleep. So, if you want to avoid this, you should eat your last meal at least two to three hours before bed.

Now, I know all of this might sound like a lot of work, but trust me, it's worth it. Not only will you sleep better, but you'll also feel better during the day. So, next time you're tempted to scroll through your phone, or drink another cup of coffee, or chow down on a big meal, just remember: timing is everything. And if you want to reduce your daily stress, you need to avoid stimulating activities before bed.

And remember, "A good laugh and a long sleep are the best cures in the doctor's book" so try to keep things light and humorous, don't take it too seriously, and give yourself permission to relax and unwind before bed. Happy Snoozing!

101. Use a weighted blanket

Imagine being wrapped up in a warm, cozy cocoon, feeling all your worries and anxieties melt away. That's exactly what a weighted blanket can do for you.

But, you might be wondering, "How does this blanket work its magic?" The science behind it is quite simple. The gentle pressure of the blanket, also known as deep touch pressure, mimics the feeling of being hugged or swaddled. This sensation triggers the release of serotonin and melatonin, two chemicals that promote feelings of calm and relaxation.

Now, let me give you some examples of how a weighted blanket can help reduce your daily stress. Imagine you're lying in bed, trying to fall asleep but your mind is racing with thoughts of work, bills, and everything else. You toss and turn, unable to find a comfortable position. But, with a weighted blanket, you'll feel like you're being hugged by a warm, fluffy cloud, lulling you into a peaceful slumber.

Or, let's say you're feeling anxious and stressed before a big presentation at work. You can wrap yourself in a weighted blanket, take a few deep breaths, and feel the calmness wash over you. It's like having your own personal stress-relieving hug, right there in the office.

And, for those of you who love to indulge in some Netflix and chill, a weighted blanket is the perfect companion. Imagine snuggling up under its cozy embrace, binging your favorite show, and feeling all your worries disappear. It's like a warm, weighted blanket of happiness.

A weighted blanket is a simple yet effective solution to reducing daily stress. It's like having your own personal hugger, 24/7. So, go ahead and give it a try, I guarantee you'll feel the difference.

And if you don't, well, at least you'll have a really cool blanket to snuggle with.

102. Try a white noise machine

Are you tired of lying awake at night, listening to the sound of your neighbor's dog barking or the cars passing by on the street? Have you tried earplugs, but found that they just don't quite do the trick? Well, my friend, I have the solution for you: a white noise machine.

Now, you may be thinking, "But wait, isn't white noise just a bunch of static and background noise?" And to that, I say, you are both right and wrong. White noise machines don't just play static, they play a variety of soothing sounds such as the sound of the ocean, a gentle rainstorm, or even the sound of a babbling brook. These sounds work to block out external noise and create a peaceful environment for sleep.

Think of it like this: imagine you're at a loud party and you're trying to have a conversation with someone. It's pretty hard to hear them over the music and chatter, right? Now, imagine if there was a soothing background noise that was louder than the party noise. Suddenly, it's much easier to hear the person you're talking to. That's essentially how a white noise machine works. It creates a louder background noise that helps block out the external noise, making it easier for you to sleep.

But it's not just for sleep, white noise machines are also great for reducing daily stress. You can use it during your workday to help you focus, or even during yoga or meditation to help you relax.

The End is Just the Beginning

And there you have it folks, 102 original ideas to help you manage stress and stay focused. But don't just take my word for it, try out these techniques for yourself and see what works best for you. Remember, there's no one-size-fits-all solution when it comes to managing stress and staying focused. It's all about finding what works for you, and that's the beauty of this book. It's like a buffet of options, pick and choose what you like, and leave the rest.

But don't get discouraged if you don't find your "magic" technique right away, managing stress and staying focused is an ongoing process, it's not a one-time thing. It's like going to the gym, you can't just go once and expect to be in shape for the rest of your life. It takes practice, patience, and persistence. So, be kind to yourself, don't beat yourself up if you slip up, just get back on track and keep going.

This book is a tool to help you navigate the stress-filled world we live in, but it's not the end-all-be-all. It's just the beginning of your journey. So go forth, and conquer stress with a smile and a sense of humor, because sometimes the best way to deal with stress is to laugh at it.

Made in the USA
Middletown, DE
24 July 2023